Simple Home Cooking

Cupcakes

Publisher's Note: Raw or semi-cooked eggs should not be consumed by babies, toddlers, pregnant or breastfeeding women, the elderly or those suffering from a chronic illness.

Publisher & Creative Director: Nick Wells
Senior Project Editor: Marcus Hardy
Art Director: Mike Spender
Layout Design: Jane Ashley
Digital Design & Production: Chris Herbert
Proofreader: Dawn Laker

Special thanks to Lydia Good for editorial assistance.

Special thanks also to Digby Smith and Helen Wall, and to the following for supplying materials for photography:

For all cake-decorating supplies by mail order, such as paper cases, sugarpaste, fondant, icing colours and equipment and bakeware:
Squires Group, Squires House, 3 Waverley Lane, Farnham Surrey, GU9 8BB. Tel: 0845 22 55 67 1/2. www.squire-shop.com
For bakeware, trays and paper cases by mail order:
Lakeland, Alexandria Buildings, Windermere, Cumbria, LA23 1BQ. Tel: 01539 488 100

This is a **FLAME TREE** Book

FLAME TREE PUBLISHING
Crabtree Hall, Crabtree Lane
Fulham, London SW6 6TY
United Kingdom
www.flametreepublishing.com

First published 2012

Simple Home Cooking

Cupcakes

**FLAME TREE
PUBLISHING**

Contents

Ingredients and

Equipment

Why are cupcakes so popular? They seem to be on sale everywhere these days, but, as these little cakes are so quick and easy (you will find that most of the recipes in this book take under half an hour to bake), it is so simple to make your own. Cupcakes are delightful and very versatile – they are ideal for breakfast, for an informal tea, for a special occasion or for children's parties.

Introduction

In this book, you will enjoy creating your own home-made masterpieces, and also, as shop-bought cakes are expensive, you will notice the difference in price. There is no comparison to the quality of home-made cakes and the fun to be had in making and baking them. You also have plenty of scope for decorating, so you can create tailor-made treats for all sorts of occasions.

As a gift or a centrepiece, a batch of cupcakes brings a personal touch to virtually any celebration, from a flamboyant wedding anniversary to a children's party. This book has cakes for every occasion, some very quick and easy, some requiring a little more patience. You will find cakes for birthdays, or everyday cupcakes that go really well with a simple cup of tea. And some of these sweet ideas are absolutely ideal for packing away into lunchboxes.

Baking is a good way to introduce children to the art of cookery and these recipes will help to teach the basic techniques. Children also love the decorating part, and there are lots of ideas here to choose from.

If you are ever asked to bake for a charity stall or school fête, cupcakes are the quick and easy choice that will not break your budget. In case you are short on time, this book includes tips on preparing ahead and freezing to make life easy.

So what is the best part of baking cupcakes? Well, they give so much pleasure: you get a real sense of satisfaction when you

create a fresh batch of delicious bakes, accompanied by the marvellous aroma of baking that fills your home; and just watch the delighted reaction when you give them to your friends and neighbours.

This book is aimed at both those new to baking and experienced bakers, and shows how to create these popular mini cakes, from the right equipment and ingredients to the cake and its decoration. So choose a recipe that appeals, get out your mixing bowls and start baking!

How to Use This Book

If you are a first-time or less experienced baker, remember that there are no secrets to baking – just follow our simple step-by-step guides to ensure successful results. The choice is yours – you can make deep cakes, shallower cupcakes, and delicate fairy cakes or mini cakes. The size of each of your cakes will depend on the depth of your trays and how deeply you fill the paper cases.

Everybody loves home bakes and friends always welcome old favourites, but everyone loves to try new treats. This book is divided into sections that deal with different types of cakes, including family favourites and fairy cakes for teatime treats, luscious chocolate cakes, and small cakes decorated for special occasions such as birthdays, Mothers' Day, weddings and Christmas.

Baking and cake decoration involves many different techniques and a little skill is needed for certain cakes, but you will build up your confidence through practice. To help you achieve success every time, there are tips on choosing the right type of cupcake and bun trays, and paper liners. Using the very best ingredients you can find is also extremely important, as are your utensils and careful weighing and measuring. You will not achieve good results without first checking your oven for correct temperature settings and exact timings.

All methods and techniques in this book are clearly explained with plenty of step-by-step photographs to help you achieve good results and you will find a set of patterns and templates at the back of this book to trace round onto clear greaseproof paper. These can be transferred to rolled-out icing by tracing round the pattern onto the icing with the tip of a sharp knife.

Check Your Oven

Each recipe begins with an oven setting, and it is important to preheat the oven to the correct temperature before placing the cakes in to bake. As well as preheating the oven, it is important to arrange the shelves in the correct position in the oven before you start. The best baking position for cupcakes is just above the centre of the oven and best results are achieved by baking only one tray at a time. If you bake two trays at once, you may find the lower tray will come out with flatter tops to the cakes.

Many of us have fan-assisted ovens. These circulate hot air round the oven and heat up very quickly. For fan ovens, you will need to reduce the temperature stated in the recipe by 10 per cent, which is usually 20°C. For example, if the stated temperature in a recipe is 180°C, then you need to reduce it to 160°C for a fan-assisted oven. However, ovens do vary

Introduction

according to the brand, so you should follow your manufacturer's instructions very closely and get to know the way your oven heats. If the temperature inside your oven is too high, then the outsides of the cakes will burn before the interior has had time to cook properly. If it is too cool, the cakes may sink or not rise evenly. Try not to open the oven door until at least halfway through the baking time, when the cakes have had time to rise and set, as a sudden drop in temperature at this stage will stop the cakes rising and they may sink.

Weighing and Measuring

All of the recipes in this book give metric and imperial measurements, but you must stick to one set only – i.e. only ever use either metric or imperial in one recipe, as they are not exact equivalents.

All spoon measurements should be used level (as opposed to 'heaped') for accuracy, and always use a recognised set of metric or imperial spoon measures for best results. Do not use domestic teaspoons and tablespoons as measures, as these may be deeper or shallower than a proper measuring spoon. Never estimate weights, as you will not achieve an accurate result.

Ingredients for baking should be weighed exactly and good kitchen scales are a vital piece of equipment for a baker. Old-fashioned scales with a pan and a set of weights or modern ones with a digital display screen are equally good, as long as they are accurate. A measuring jug is vital for liquids, and it needs to be marked with small measures for smaller amounts.

Equipment Needed

Trays and Cases

- **Metal Trays** – Trays come in a variety of different weights and sizes; they are generally available with six or 12 deep-set holes. When purchasing, buy the heaviest type you can – although these will be expensive, they produce the best results, as they have good heat distribution and do not buckle. Trays can vary in the size and depth of hole, which obviously affects the eventual size of the cupcakes. If using trays without a nonstick finish, it is advisable to give these a light greasing before use. To grease trays, apply a thin film of melted vegetable margarine with a pastry brush or rub round the tray with kitchen paper and a little softened butter or margarine. You will normally need to line metal trays with deep paper cases or strips of baking parchment.

- **Silicone Trays and Cases** – These are flexible and produce very good results. Although they are sold as nonstick, it is still advisable to rub round each hole or case with a little oil on kitchen paper to prevent sticking. Silicone cupcake cases come in many bright colours and, unlike paper cases, are reusable. Simply wash out any crumbs, after use, in soapy water and leave them to dry, or clean them in the dishwasher.

Equipment Needed

~ **Fairy-cake Trays** – Also known as 'bun trays' or 'patty trays', these are similar to ordinary trays but have shallower indentations for making smaller individual cakes. You will need to line each indentation with a paper fairy-cake case.

~ **Mini Trays** – These have small individual holes that are half the size of holes in bigger trays. They can be made of metal, but the silicone trays are particularly useful for mini cupcakes, as they turn out so easily and give a good shape.

~ **Paper Cases** – These come in many varieties, colours and shapes. It is advisable to buy the more expensive types, which are thicker and give a good shape to the cake as it rises. Oil and moisture is less likely to penetrate the thicker cases, whereas it may show through the cheaper ones. Metallic gold, silver and coloured cupcake cases give good results and create a stunning effect for a special occasion. Cupcake cases also come in mini sizes. These may not be so easy to find but can be bought from mail-order cake decoration suppliers.

Baking Papers and Foil

Nonstick baking 'parchment' or 'paper' is useful for lining the bases of small trays or for drying out chocolate and sugarpaste shapes.

Greaseproof paper is needed for making triangular paper icing bags. Baking parchment can be used, but greaseproof paper is better, as it is thinner and more flexible.

~ **Foil** – A large sheet of kitchen foil is good for wrapping cakes or for protecting wrapped cakes in the freezer.

Equipment and Utensils for Baking

- **Electric Mixers** – A handheld electric mixer makes quick work of whisking butter and sugar, and is an invaluable aid for cake baking. A large tabletop mixer is useful if you are making larger quantities of cakes and is good for whisking frostings and buttercream in larger quantities. Do not be tempted to use a food processor for mixing small amounts, as it is easy to over-process and this may produce flat cakes.

- **Mixing Bowls** – You will need a set of different size, mixing bowls for beating small and large amounts of mixture, frostings and icings.

- **Wooden Spoon** – Keep an old-fashioned, large wooden spoon aside for baking, for beating butters and creaming. Do not use one that has been used for frying savoury things such as onions, as the flavours will taint the cake mixture.

- **Measuring Spoons** – A set of standard measuring spoons for accurate measuring of small quantities of ingredients is vital. Remember that all spoon measures should be level and not to use cutlery such as kitchen tablespoons or teaspoons, as these sizes differ and may be inaccurate.

- **Cake Tester or Skewer** – Use a small, thin, metal skewer for inserting into the centre of a cake to test if the cakes are ready. This is a handy piece of equipment but, if you do not have one, a clean, thin, metal knitting needle may be used instead.

Pastry Brush – A pastry brush is used for brushing glazes over cakes and melted butter round trays. As brushes tend to wear out regularly and shed their bristles, keep a spare new brush to hand.

Palette Knives – A small and a large palette knife are ideal for many jobs, including loosening cakes from their trays, lifting cakes and swirling on buttercream icing. A palette knife with a cranked blade is useful for lifting small cakes or flat pieces of sugarpaste.

Kitchen Scissors – Scissors are essential for many small jobs, including cutting papers to size and snipping cherries, dried fruits or nuts into chunks.

Grater – A grater is useful for grating citrus zests, chocolate and marzipan. Choose one with a fine and a coarse side.

Sieves – Use a large wire sieve for sifting flour and dry ingredients together and keep a smaller one, ideally nylon, aside just for icing sugars.

Wire Racks – Racks are vital to allow air to circulate round the hot cakes to let them cool down quickly, which prevents them from becoming moist or soggy underneath.

Stamps and Cutters – Stamps and cutters of almost any imaginable shape can be bought from specialist cake and baking stores. They come in classic metal cookie-cutter styles, in plastic, or as plunger-style. If you do not have appropriate cutters, there are some templates at the back of this book that can be used instead.

Piping Bags and Nozzles – A nylon piping bag that comes with a set of five nozzles is a very useful piece of equipment for decorating with icings. Look for a set with a plain nozzle and various star nozzles for piping swirls round cupcakes. The larger the star nozzle, the wider the swirls will be on the finished cakes. Disposable paper or clear plastic icing bags are available, but nylon piping bags can be washed out in warm soapy water and dried out, ready to re-use again and again.

To Make a Paper Icing Bag – Cut out a 38 x 25.5 cm/15 x 10 inch rectangle of greaseproof paper. Fold it diagonally in half to form two triangular shapes. Cut along the fold line to make two triangles. One of these triangles can be used another time – it is quicker and easier to make two at a time from one square than to measure and mark out a triangle on a sheet of paper.

Fold one of the points on the long side of the triangle over the top to make a sharp cone and hold in the centre. Fold the other sharp end of the triangle over the cone.

Hold all the points together at the back of the cone, keeping the pointed end sharp. Turn the points inside the top edge, fold over to make a crease, then secure with a piece of sticky tape.

To use, snip away the end, place a piping nozzle in position and fill the bag with icing, or fill the bag with icing first, then snip away a tiny hole at the end for piping a plain edge, writing or piping tiny dots.

Equipment Needed

Ingredients

In baking, most cakes are made by mixing sugar, fats, flour and eggs together. During the mixing, air is incorporated into the mixture to greater or lesser degrees to make it rise during baking. As a cake mixture bakes, the strands of gluten in the flour are stretched and the heat hardens them to give a light sponge-like texture.

Sugar

Sugar is not just included to give sweetness to cakes. It also produces a structure and texture that makes cakes tender, so always choose the correct type for your recipe.

- **Granulated Sugar** – This is the standard sugar that you add to your tea. It comes in white and golden unrefined varieties and is used for toppings. The coarseness of granulated sugar means that it does not dissolve easily and is not designed for most baking recipes, so is no good for the creaming method.

- **Caster Sugar** – This is a fine-ground granulated sugar, which also comes in white and golden (or 'natural') unrefined varieties. It blends easily with butter and margarine when beaten or 'creamed' into light sponge mixtures.

- **Soft Light and Dark Brown Sugars** – These cream well and are usually used in richer cakes or spicy fruit mixtures such as carrot cake, and in recipes where rich colour and flavour are needed. Store this sugar in a tightly sealed container to prevent it from drying out. If it does become dry or lumpy, pound it back into crystals with the flat end of a rolling pin before you use it.

- **Muscovado** – This sugar is natural and unrefined, with a deep brown colour and rich flavour that makes fruit cakes and gingerbreads extra special. It comes in light and dark varieties.

- **Demerara Sugar** – Demerara sugar is golden in colour and has a lumpy, grainy texture. It is too coarse for creaming, but is often used for recipes where sugar is melted or as a sparkly topping.

- **Golden Syrup, Honey, Treacle and Molasses** – These are thick, liquid sugars. They can be used in cakes made by the melting method but, as they tend to burn at high temperatures, these cakes need to be cooked on a lower heat.

Eggs

- **Storing** – Always store eggs in the refrigerator, but remove them an hour or so before you start to bake, as better results will be achieved if you allow them to reach room temperature before using. This is because, at this temperature, eggs will whisk better and achieve more aeration.

Ingredients

This not only gives more volume to the mixture, but also allows the eggs to blend in more easily. Cold eggs used straight from the refrigerator can curdle or split a mixture.

⁓ Egg Types – Eggs sold as 'value' or 'economy' can be used for baking cupcakes, particularly if you are working to a budget (but do not forget the welfare issues involved in this choice). Also, do remember that these may be ungraded and of different sizes, so, for best results, buy eggs marked as 'medium' and 'large'. If you do use economy eggs, make sure to note the sizes you are using and try to even out the quantity by, say, using 1 large and 2 small eggs instead of 3 medium-sized ones.

⁓ Egg Powder – Dried egg-white powder gives good results and can be substituted in royal icing recipes, or in recipes where you are unsure about using raw egg whites in the case of the very young, pregnant women or the elderly.

⁓ Separating Eggs – When separating whites from their yolks, break them into a cup one at a time so that, if there are any specks of yolk or pieces of shell in the cup, you can easily remove them. If yolk is present in a bowl of whites, it will prevent whisking – even a tiny speck of yolk will stop the whites from whisking into foam and you will have wasted the mixture.

Yogurt

Plain yogurt is great for adding to some cakes, as it adds richness and moisture. Do not use low-fat yogurt – stick to plain, thickset natural yogurts that have far more substance to them.

Buttermilk

Buttermilk is produced by adding bacteria to low-fat milk to thicken and sour it. This is used in recipes for small cakes that use bicarbonate of soda, as the acidity from the buttermilk produces carbon dioxide, which raises the cakes. Buttermilk will give an extra lift to cupcakes, as well as a far richer flavour. You will find buttermilk on sale in the dairy section of larger supermarkets but, if it is not available, use 1 tablespoon lemon juice to 300 ml/11 fl oz plain yogurt or whole milk as a substitute.

Flours

Plain white flour provides the structure of a cake, but contains nothing to make a cake rise, so cakes that do not need raising agents are made with plain flour. Most recipes using plain flour have bicarbonate of soda or baking powder added to them to make the cakes rise. It is always advisable to sift this into the mixture to incorporate the raising agents evenly.

- Self-raising Flour – This type of flour has raising agents already added, that will add air to make a cake rise, so is used for light sponge mixtures. If you have only plain flour available, then add $2^{1}/_{2}$ tsp baking powder to 225 g/8 oz plain flour to turn it into a self-raising flour.

- Wholemeal Flour – Wholemeal (sometimes 'wholewheat', or 'brown') flours contain bran from the wheat. This gives a good texture with extra fibre, and it tends to keep cupcakes moist and gives a mellow flavour. If you want to substitute wholemeal flour for white in a recipe, you will need to add extra liquid, as the bran in wholemeal flour will absorb more fluid (hence why the cakes are more moist).

Ingredients

Storing Flour – White flours should be stored in a cool, dry place for up to 6 months, but wholemeal flours will not keep as long, as they have a higher fat content, so check the use-by date on all packs. Flour is best stored in a sealed airtight container. Always wash and dry this thoroughly before refilling and never add new flour to old. Small micro-organisms will form in very old flour, from the protein, and these can be seen as tiny black specks that will spread into new flour. If you do not have a container, store the opened paper bag inside a large plastic bag and make sure all flour is kept dry. Damp flour weighs more and therefore alters the recipe, which could lead to heavy or flat cakes.

Raising Agents

Raising agents are added to flour to make cakes rise and produce a light texture. It is important to be accurate when measuring these fine powders out, so always use a measuring spoon.

Baking Powder – This is a mixture of bicarbonate of soda and cream of tartar. When liquid is added, the powder fizzes and bubbles and produces carbon dioxide, which expands with heat during baking and gives an airy texture. Take care not to use very hot or boiling liquid in mixtures, as these can reduce the power of baking powder.

Bicarbonate of Soda – This is a gentler raising agent and is often used to give melted or spicy mixtures a lift. Cakes will have a bitter flavour if too much is added, so measure this out carefully and accurately with a proper measuring spoon, not a domestic teaspoon.

Fats

Fat adds structure, texture and flavour to cakes and improves their keeping qualities. Always remove them from the refrigerator before using them – they are easier to mix in when at room temperature.

- **Butter and Hard Block Margarine** – Butter and hard margarine can be interchanged in a recipe, and the results will be the same. Butter, however, will always give a better flavour to cupcakes and so, if they are for a special occasion, is it well worth spending a little extra on this.

- **Soft Margarine** – Sold in tubs, this is wonderful for using in all-in-one sponge recipes where all the ingredients are quickly mixed together in one bowl. This fat always produces good results and is quick and easy to use because it does not have to be used at room temperature but can be taken straight from the refrigerator. Do not substitute soft margarine for butter or hard block margarine in a recipe, as it is a totally different kind of fat, which will not produce the same results. Cupcakes using soft margarine usually require extra raising agent, so do follow the recipe carefully and do not be tempted to over-beat the mixture, as it will become wet and the cakes may sink. Up to 2 minutes' whisking with an electric mixer is fine to make a smooth mixture.

Ingredients

Dried Fruits

∾ **Dried Vine Fruits** – Fruits such as raisins, currants, sultanas and cranberries (pictured left) are usually sold ready-washed and prepared for baking, but it is still worth looking through them for pieces of stalk and grit before baking. Dried cranberries, sometimes sold as 'craisins', add a sweet, fresh flavour to cakes, similar to dried cherries. As they are bright red in colour, these can be used as a topping or decoration, as well as baked into mixtures. Fresh cranberries also make a colourful cake decoration.

∾ **Glacé Cherries** – Sold thinly coated in syrup, these come in a dark maroon, natural colour and a brighter red colour (pictured left), the latter usually being cheaper than the natural variety. These cherries keep well stored in their tubs in a cool place. Always wash the syrup off the cherries before baking, as it will cause the cherries to sink into the mixture.

∾ **Cherries** – These are semi-sweet and are about the size of sultanas. Dried morello cherries have a bittersweet flavour and are delicious added to cupcake recipes.

∾ **Ginger** – Ginger comes in a sticky glacé variety or in a dried crystallised form (pictured left), coated in sugar crystals. Use both varieties chopped and added to recipes or chop and use with a drizzle icing for an attractive cake topping.

∽ Angelica – A bright green, crystallised stem from a herb, this can be chopped into pieces and added to mixtures or scattered over cakes to provide a pretty, colourful topping. It needs to be rinsed and dried before use to wash away the sugary coating and reveal the bright green colour. Store it tightly wrapped in a plastic bag inside a sealed container to keep it fresh and flexible.

∽ Citrus Peels – Bright and colourful, these add a zesty tang to recipes. Dried orange, lemon and lime peels can be bought as whole large pieces (pictured right) in syrup or a sugar glaze, or ready–chopped into small pieces coated in light syrup in a tub (often sold as 'mixed peel'). Keep both varieties in a cool place to prevent crystallisation or drying out of the fruit.

∽ Dried Banana – Dried banana chips (pictured right) make very pretty cake toppings, while semi-dried or soft banana chips can be chopped finely and added to cake mixtures.

∽ Dried Pineapple – Pineapple for baking comes in many varieties. Soft dried pineapple (pictured right) is sold in thin, delicate slices or fans in vacuum-sealed packs and has an intense concentrated flavour, so only use small amounts, chopped into mixtures. These delicate fans make a pretty topping for individual cakes. Keep stored in an airtight container, as the fruits tend to soften once the packs are opened. Use drained canned pineapple rings or chunks for chopping and adding to cake mixtures.

Ingredients

Dried Apricots – Dried apricots are richer and sweeter than the fresh fruits. Some dried apricots are shrivelled and have a dark brown colour and these need soaking before use. Look for packs of the ready-to-eat varieties (pictured left), which are soft and moist and ready to use for baking. Organic dried apricots usually have a brighter orange colour and a better flavour, so are worth looking out for.

Dried Coconut – Coconut comes in many varieties. Powdery desiccated coconut comes in fine and sweetened varieties and can be used in mixtures for natural sweetness or as a coating or topping for cupcakes. Dried coconut slices (pictured left) are large, sweet wedges, which make a stunning cake topping, or smaller, thin-cut coconut chips, in natural or toasted varieties, which make a great topping pressed into white buttercream.

Prunes – Prunes are dried plums, which add sweetness and richness to baking. Look for packs of ready-to-eat pitted prunes, which means they have the stones removed and are ready for chopping.

Dried Figs – Figs are sold as dried, which need to be soaked overnight in hot water, or ready-to-eat (pictured left), and these are plump and moist and ideal for chopping and adding to mixtures.

Dried Dates – Dates are sold in dried blocks, which need to be soaked in warm water before use, or as semi-dried or soft, ready-to-eat dates, which can be used straight away for adding sweetness to mixtures.

Fresh Fruits

Fresh fruits, such as bananas, citrus fruits and berries, all make great additions to cupcake recipes. They can be baked into the mixture for natural sweetness and flavour or used as decorative toppings. Cupcakes topped with fresh fruits will need to be refrigerated and eaten on the day of decorating.

Spices

Most dried spices have a reasonably long shelf life, but will not keep indefinitely, and remember that they will gradually lose their aroma and flavour. It is a good idea to buy in small quantities only when you need them. You will find that both light and heat affect the power and flavour of spices, so, if stored in clear glass jars, keep them out of the light – the best place to store spices is in a dark, cool, dry place.

Nuts

Using nuts in baking is more expensive, so, since they deteriorate quickly, it is especially important not to buy them in large quantities. If you buy a large bargain pack of nuts that you are not going to use immediately, store the extra ones in the freezer, where they will keep for up to 6 months. The flavour of nuts, particularly hazelnuts, is always improved by toasting for a few minutes before use. The easiest way to do this is to place them in a single layer on a foil-lined baking tray and grill them lightly.

- Almonds – Almonds can be bought in whole, blanched, flaked, chopped or ground varieties. Shelled almonds will still have their skins on, so, to remove these, immerse the nuts in boiling water for 2–3 minutes, then plunge into cold water and the skins will slip away easily.

Ingredients

Ground almonds have a powdery texture and can be added straight into mixtures to give structure and moistness to a recipe. If you do not have ground almonds available, place whole or flaked almonds in a food processor and grind to a coarse powder. Take extra care not to overgrind the almonds, however, as too fine a powder will release the natural oils from the nuts.

Hazelnuts – Hazelnuts are sold as whole, skinned or unskinned and ground. For the best flavour in cakes, choose whole skinned nuts and quickly toast them under a grill, then rub away the skins. Chop or grind and use immediately.

Walnuts – Since walnuts (pictured left) contain more oil than other nuts, they will turn rancid quickly, so do not buy these in bulk. Packs of whole nuts or halves are far more expensive, so, if you need chopped walnuts in a cupcake recipe, buy the cheaper packs sold as walnut pieces, which are equally good.

Pecans – Pecan nuts (pictured left) are sweet and richly flavoured, with a far superior taste to other types of nut, but tend to be more expensive. One whole nut or a few chopped pieces will make an ideal luxury topping for a cake.

Peanuts – Peanuts can be used, coarsely chopped, for mixing into a variety of cakes and as a crunchy topping for cake mixtures. Choose ordinary salted peanuts, sold in foil bags, which, surprisingly, tend to have the best flavour.

Flavourings

Flavouring extracts (pictured right) are very concentrated and usually sold in liquid form in small bottles. A teaspoon measure will usually be enough to flavour a cake mixture for around 12 cakes.

Vanilla and almond extracts are ideal to impart their delicate flavours into cake mixtures and you will find the more expensive extracts give a finer and more natural flavour. Rosewater can be used for flavouring both cake mixtures and icings and has a delicate, perfumed flavour. Fruit flavourings, such as lemon, lime, orange and raspberry, will give a fresh twist to mixtures and icings.

Chocolate

For the best results and a professional finish and flavour, it is always advisable to buy the highest-quality chocolate you can find, although this will be more expensive. Better-quality chocolates contain a higher percentage of real cocoa fat, which gives a flavour and texture far superior to cheaper varieties. (Cheaper chocolate labelled as 'cooking' or 'baking' chocolate contains a much smaller percentage of cocoa solids and is best avoided in favour of better-quality eating chocolate.)

Ingredients

The amount of cocoa fat or solids contained in chocolate will be marked on the wrapper of any good-quality chocolate. Those marked as 70-per-cent cocoa solids will give the best results and you will find this chocolate is shiny and brittle and it should snap very easily.

❧ **Dark Chocolate** – Also known as 'plain' or 'plain dark' chocolate, this is the most useful all-purpose type of chocolate for baking, as it has a good, strong flavour.

❧ **Milk Chocolate** – Milk chocolate has sugar added and is sweeter than dark, so is good for melting for icings and decorations.

❧ **White Chocolate** – This is not strictly chocolate, as it contains only cocoa butter, milk and sugar. It is expensive and the most difficult to work with, so must be used with care. It is best to grate it finely and keep the temperature very low when melting it.

❧ **Chocolate Cake Covering** – This is a cheaper substitute containing a minimum of 2.5 percent cocoa solids and vegetable oil. It is considerably cheaper than real chocolate and the flavour is not as good, but it is easy to melt and sets quickly and well for a coating.

❧ **Chocolate Chips** – Chips come in dark, milk and white varieties and are sold in small bags. They are useful for adding to cupcake mixtures to enrich them and add a delicious texture as they part-melt into the cakes on baking.

~ Cocoa Powder – Cocoa powder needs to be cooked to release the full flavour, so blend it with boiling water to make into a paste, then cool before adding to a recipe, or sift it into the bowl with the flour.

~ Drinking Chocolate – Be aware that this is not the same as cocoa powder, as it contains milk powder and sugar. Some recipes may specify using drinking chocolate and these are successful, but do not substitute it for cocoa powder, as it will spoil the flavour of a cake.

For Decorating

~ Icing Sugar – Icing sugar is fine and powdery. It is usually sold plain and white, but can also be bought as an unrefined golden (or 'natural') variety. Use it for delicate icings, frostings and decorations. Store this sugar in a dry place, as it can absorb moisture and this will make it go hard and lumpy. Always sift this sugar at least once, or preferably twice, before you use it, to remove any hard lumps that would prevent icing from achieving a smooth texture – lumpy icing is impossible to pipe out.

~ Fondant Icing Sugar – This is sold in plain and flavoured varieties and gives a beautiful glossy finish to cake toppings. Just add a little boiled water to the sugar, according to the packet instructions, to make a shiny icing that can be

Ingredients

poured or drizzled over cupcakes to give a very professional finish. Colour the plain white icing with a few spots of paste food colouring to achieve your desired result.

Flavoured fondant icing sugar is sold in strawberry, raspberry, orange, lemon and blackcurrant flavours and also has colouring added. These sugars are ideal if you want to make a large batch of cakes with different coloured and flavoured toppings. Flavoured fondant sugars can also be whisked with softened unsalted butter or cream cheese to make delicious frostings in just a few moments.

∾ Royal Icing Sugar – Royal icing sets to a classic, firm Christmas-cake-style covering. Sold in packs as plain white sugar, this is whisked with cold water to give an instant royal icing. It has dried egg white included in the mixture, so does not need the long beating that traditional royal icing recipes require. It is also ideal to use for those who cannot eat raw egg whites.

∾ Tubes of Writing Icing – You can buy small tubes of ready-coloured royal icing or gel icing, usually in sets of black, red, yellow and blue, and these are ideal for small amounts of writing or for piping on dots or small decorations.

∾ Food Colourings – You can buy food colourings in liquid, paste, gel and powder or dust forms in a great range of colours.

Paste food colourings are best for using with sugarpaste. These are sold in small tubs and are very concentrated, so should be added to the sugarpaste dot by dot on the end of a wooden cocktail stick. Knead the colouring in evenly, adding more until you get the colour you require.

Liquid and gel food colourings are ideal for adding to frostings. Add this cautiously drop by drop, beating the frosting well until you reach the colour you require.

Dusts and sparkle colourings should be lightly brushed onto dry sugarpaste to form a delicate sheen to decorations such as flowers.

◦ Bought Sugar Decorations and Sprinkles – A range of sprinkles can be bought in supermarkets or by mail order from specialist cake decorating companies, and these provide a wonderful way to make quick and easy cake toppings.

Sweets can be used in baking cupcakes, such as the crushed peppermint sweets used in the Mint Choc Chip Cupcakes (*see* page 122), but of course they also make excellent decorations to go on top too. If you have decorated a cupcake with buttercream or cream cheese frosting, why not simply pick complimentary colours of sweets and place on top. If you're decorating cupcakes with children, perhaps at a birthday party or just as something fun to do together, this is something easy for them to use.

Ingredients

Basic Techniques

Preparing Trays

When recipes give instructions on how to prepare and line trays, these are important steps, so do not be tempted to skimp on these. The time and expense in baking cupcakes may be wasted if, at the end of cooking, they will not turn out of the tray properly.

Measuring Ingredients

Measuring dry ingredients when baking is very important, too much or too little of any ingredient can change the end result quite substantially. This applies especially to raising agents like baking powder, bicarbonate of soda and cream of tartar. It is a good idea to invest in a set of cooks measuring spoons and remember to use either metric or Imperial measurements. Do not mix the two when weighing out the ingredients.

Different Making Methods

∾ Creaming – Light cakes are made by the creaming method, which means that the butter and sugar are first beaten or 'creamed' together.

A little care is needed for this method. Use a large mixing bowl to beat the fat and sugar together until pale and fluffy. The eggs are gradually beaten in to form a slackened batter and the flour is folded in last, to stiffen up the mixture.

In some recipes, egg whites are whisked and added to the mixture separately for extra lightness.

When the eggs are added, they are best used at room temperature to prevent the mixture from splitting or 'curdling'. Adding a teaspoon of flour with each beaten egg will help to keep the mixture light and smooth and prevent the mixture from separating. A badly mixed, curdled batter will hold less air and be heavy or can cause a sunken cake.

Place a folded tea towel under the mixing bowl if creaming or mixing your cupcake mixture by hand. This stops the bowl slipping around and makes the whole operation quicker and easier.

Rubbing In – In this method, the fat is lightly worked into the flour between the fingers, as in pastry making, until the mixture resembles fine crumbs. This can be done by hand or in a food processor. Enough liquid is stirred in to give a soft mixture that will drop easily from a spoon. This method is used for easy fruitcakes and small buns such as rock cakes.

Basic Techniques

~ **All-In-One Mixtures** – This 'one-stage' method is quick and easy and is perfect for those new to baking, as it does not involve any complicated techniques. It is ideal for making light sponges, but soft tub-type margarine or softened butter at room temperature must be used.

There is no need for any creaming or rubbing in, as all the ingredients are simply placed in a large bowl and quickly beaten together for just a few minutes until smooth.

Take care not to overbeat, as this will make the mixture too wet. Self-raising flour with the addition of a little extra baking powder is vital for a good rise.

~ **The Melting Method** – Cakes with a delicious moist, sticky texture, such as gingerbread, are made by this method. These cakes use a high proportion of sugar and syrup, which are gently warmed together in a saucepan with the fat, until the sugar granules have dissolved and the mixture is liquid.

It is important to cool the hot melted mixture a little before beating in flour, eggs and spices to make a batter, otherwise it will damage the power of the raising agent.

Bicarbonate of soda is often used as a raising agent in this method, to help raise a heavy batter.

These cakes benefit from storing for at least a day before cutting, to make them moist and sticky.

❧ Fruit-cakes – Rich fruit-cakes are usually made by the creaming method, then dried fruits and nuts are folded into the mixture last.

Checking to See if the Cakes Are Cooked

Serving up uncooked cupcakes would be a disaster so make sure you check whether they have been properly cooked before decorating. Small cupcakes should be golden, risen and firm to the touch when pressed lightly in the centre. The last part of a cupcake to cook is the centre, so, after the baking time stated in the recipes, you should check this area.

For light, sponge-type cakes, press the centre lightly with the fingertips and, if the cake is cooked, it should spring back easily. To test more thoroughly, insert a thin, warmed skewer into the deepest part of the centre.

If the cake is cooked, it will come out perfectly cleanly, with no mixture sticking to it, but, if there is some on the skewer, then bake the cakes for a little longer and test again.

❧   Basic Techniques

Once They're Done

Cooling the Cakes

All freshly baked cakes are very fragile; they need time to stand in the trays to cool for a short time to make them firm.

- Sponges and delicate cupcakes need standing time of about 2 minutes.

- If your cakes start to stick to their moulds, leave them until the cakes are firm, then loosen their sides by running round the trays with a small palette knife. Then, very carefully, turn the cakes out on a wire rack so they can cool down.

- Do not leave cupcakes in paper cases in the bun trays to cool completely, as moisture that collects in the bun trays will cause the paper cases to go damp and discolour.

What Went Wrong and Why?

- **Why Did They Sink?** – It is important to weigh and measure all the ingredients correctly. If you add too much raising agent, such as baking powder or bicarbonate of soda, this can make the cakes sink. Or cakes can sink in the middle if the mixture was too wet, which can be caused by overbeating when using soft margarine or adding too much liquid. Opening or slamming the oven door during the baking time can also cause cakes to sink.

❧ **Why Has it Not Cooked Fully?** – The use of the correct size of tray is important; if the tray is too small, then the mixture will not cook through properly. This will also happen if the oven is too cool and the cake is under-baked.

❧ **What Caused a Heavy Texture?** – The reason for this is usually using too little raising agent, but small cakes can also be close and heavy by adding too much fat, egg or flour. If the mixture is too dry or too wet, it will affect the texture, as will undermixing – that is, if the cake is not beaten sufficiently to add air, the texture will be coarse.

❧ **What Caused a Dry Texture?** – Small cakes with a dry texture tend to be crumbly when cut and go stale rapidly. This can be caused if the cakes were baked too slowly or contain too much raising agent. The mixture may also be too dry if not rubbed in or beaten sufficiently.

❧ **What Caused a Crack or Peak in the Top of the Cake?** – If the trays contain too much mixture, the batter will rise up and the tops will form peaks. Baking in an oven that is too hot or baking the cakes too near the heat at the top of the oven will also cause this to happen. A mixture that is too wet or too dry will also form a cracked surface.

❧ Once They're Done

What Causes a Dark, Hard Outer Crust? – Small cakes with a hard, dark outer crust are usually baked in too hot an oven or overbaked in a fan-assisted oven at a high temperature. If you are using a fan-assisted oven, you will usually need to turn the temperature down by 20°C or follow your instruction booklet.

Why Did the Fruit Sink? – All vine fruits must be dry when added to the mixture. Glacé cherries must be washed of their syrup, dried and tossed in flour to prevent sinking. If the mixture is too wet or contains too much raising agent, the fruit will sink. Using too cool an oven or opening the oven door too soon before the end of the baking time can cause fruit to sink.

Why Do Cakes Stick to the Tray? – You will not be able to turn the cakes out of a tray if it was not greased sufficiently into all the corners. Cheap or poor-quality trays tend to produce bad results and can buckle in the heat, causing misshapen cakes.

Why Do Small Cakes Spread? – Small cakes spread out if the mixture is too wet or there is too much mixture in each case. Adding too much or too little raising agent will also cause small cakes to flatten out, as will baking in too cool an oven.

Why Are There Large Air Bubbles in the Centres of the Cakes? – Holes in cakes or an uneven texture is caused by undermixing when adding the flour or liquid. If the mixture is too dry, it will tend to contain pockets of air. If the flour and raising agent are not sieved in or properly mixed together, this can also cause air bubbles in the mixture.

- ∽ **Why Did the Cakes Not Rise?** – This is caused by not adding enough raising agent or overbeating a mixture and knocking out the air. If a mixture is too stiff and does not contain enough liquid, or is baked in too cool an oven, this will not help the cakes rise.

- ∽ **Why Do the Paper Cases Have Brown Marks?** – Take care when filling the paper cases with cake batter, as, if you spill the mixture onto the edges or outsides of the cases, it will cook and burn into dark brown marks that cannot be removed.

How to Patch Up Mistakes

- ∽ If your cakes have peaked, then these can easily be trimmed flat when the cakes are cold.

- ∽ If the cakes have overcooked or are burnt on the outside, simply scrape this away with a serrated knife and cover the surface with buttercream.

- ∽ If the cakes are a little dry, sprinkle them with a few drops of sweet sherry or orange juice.

Cutting the Tops Level

Many cupcakes form a small peak while baking and this is ideal for coating with buttercream or piping round a swirl of cream cheese frosting. However, some methods of decorating cakes require a flat surface, so, for these, trim the tops level with a knife. Coat with apricot glaze and press on a disc of almond paste or sugarpaste to give a flat surface to decorate.

Storing Cupcakes

- Ensure cakes are completely cold before storing, otherwise condensation may form and cause cakes to go mouldy.

- Large, flat, plastic food containers are ideal for cupcakes, as they enable the cakes to be kept flat in one single layer and will keep small cakes moist. Old-fashioned cake tins can be used, but they do not hold a large number of small cakes.

- If you do not have a large cake container, invert a large mixing bowl over the cakes on a plate or flat surface and the cakes will stay fresh.

- Sponge fairy-cakes will keep for 3–4 days, and richer fruitcakes for 5 days to a week.

- Cakes with fresh cream fillings and decorations need to be kept in the refrigerator and are best eaten on the day of filling with cream.

- Store cakes with sugarpaste decorations in a cool place, but not in the refrigerator. The moisture in a refrigerator will be absorbed by the sugarpaste and make this icing go limp and soggy.

- Once completely cooled, undecorated cupcakes can be frozen for up to three months by wrapping carefully in several layers of cling film or foil and placing within a freezer bag.

Transporting

To carry cupcakes to a special event, you will need to use a large, flat, plastic-lidded box. These are ideal and you will find the best boxes are those that stack into each other for ease of carrying. Special cupcake carrying sets are now on sale with a divided base that holds 12 cakes, with raised discs that the cupcakes can sit in, so that they do not move around. A plastic lid with a handle makes these boxes easy to carry. If you do not have special plastic boxes or carriers, replace the cakes in the baking trays to protect them, especially if they are decorated, and place the trays in shallow cardboard boxes for transportation.

Freezing Cupcakes

Most cupcakes will freeze well, but, for best results, freeze undecorated. Completely cool each cake and freeze in one layer on a baking sheet or flat tray. Once frozen, place in strong freezer bags or boxes and seal, to exclude as much air as possible, label and freeze.

Cakes containing fresh fruits such as blueberries or raspberries will not freeze well, as the fruit tends to make the cakes soggy when thawed, so these are best eaten fresh on the day of baking.

Thawing and Warming

To use frozen cakes, completely unwrap and thaw at room temperature on racks. The paper cases may peel away from frozen cakes, so these may need to be replaced with fresh ones before decorating the cakes.

Once They're Done

Decorating Techniques

ざ

Using Chocolate

∽ **Melting Chocolate** – Care and attention is needed to melt chocolate for baking and cake decorating needs. If the chocolate gets too hot or comes into contact with water or steam, it will 'seize' or stiffen and form into a hard ball instead of a smooth melted mixture. You can add a little vegetable oil or margarine, a teaspoon at a time, to the mixture to make it liquid again.

To melt chocolate, break the bar into small pieces, or grate or chop it, and place in a heatproof bowl standing over a bowl of warm, not hot, water. Make sure the bowl containing the chocolate is completely dry and that steam or water cannot enter the bowl. Heat the water to a gentle simmer only and leave the bowl to stand for about 5 minutes. Do not let the water get too hot or the chocolate will reach too high a temperature and will lose its sheen.

The microwave oven is ideal for melting chocolate. Place the chocolate pieces in a small microwave-proof bowl and melt gently on low or defrost settings in small bursts of 30 seconds, checking and stirring in between, until the chocolate has melted.

∽ **Making Chocolate Decorations** – *Curls and shavings* Spread melted chocolate out thinly onto a clean, dry surface such as a plastic board, marble or a clean worktop. Leave the chocolate until almost set, then pull a long, sharp-bladed knife through it at an angle to form curls or shavings. Place the curls in a lidded plastic box in the refrigerator until needed for decoration.

Leaves Wash and dry holly or rose leaves and place on a sheet of nonstick baking parchment. Melt the chocolate and paint on the underside of each leaf. Leave to dry out, then carefully peel away the leaf. You will find the veined side is uppermost on the chocolate leaf. Place in a lidded container and keep refrigerated until needed for decoration.

Crystallising Petals, Flowers, Leaves and Berries

Wash and dry herbs and leaves such as rosemary sprigs and small bay leaves, or berries such as cranberries. Separate edible petals from small flowers such as rosebuds and clean small flowers such as violets with a clean brush, but do not wash them.

Beat 1 medium egg white with 2 teaspoons cold water until frothy. Paint a thin layer of egg white carefully over the items, then sprinkle lightly with caster sugar, shaking to remove any excess. Leave to dry on a wire rack lined with nonstick baking parchment.

Decorating Techniques

Using Buttercream and Cream Cheese Frosting

These soft icings can be swirled onto the tops of cupcakes with a small palette knife or placed in a piping bag fitted with a star nozzle to pipe impressive whirls.

∾ Do not be mean with the amount of frosting you use. If this is scraped on thinly, you will see the cake underneath, so be generous.

∾ Keep cupcakes with frostings in a cool place, or refrigerate, as they contain a high percentage of butter, which will melt easily in too warm a place.

∾ Cakes coated in buttercream can be decorated easily with colourful sprinkles and sugars. To make this easy, place the sprinkles in a small saucer or on a piece of nonstick baking parchment and roll the outside edges of each cake in the decorations.

Using Sugarpaste

Sugarpaste is a versatile icing, as it can be used for covering small cakes or modelling all sorts of fancy decorations. To use as a covering, roll out the sugarpaste thinly on a surface dusted with icing sugar and cut out circles the size of the cake tops. Coat each cake with a little apricot glaze or buttercream and press on the circles to form a flat surface.

To Copy Patterns from the Templates – At the back of this book, you will find templates for some of the shapes that follow and as used in this book. Trace the pattern you want onto a sheet of clear greaseproof paper or nonstick baking parchment. Roll out the sugarpaste thinly, then position the traced pattern. Mark over the pattern with the tip of a small, sharp knife or a pin. Remove the paper and cut out the marked-on pattern with a small, sharp knife.

Making Flat Decorations – To make letters, numbers or flat decorations, roll out the sugarpaste thinly and cut out the shapes. Leave to dry on nonstick baking parchment on a flat surface or a tray for 2–3 hours to make them firm and easy to handle.

Making Roses – Colour the sugarpaste icing with pink paste food colouring. Take a small piece of sugarpaste and make a small cone shape, then roll a small pea-sized piece of sugarpaste into a ball. Flatten out the ball into a petal shape and wrap this round the cone shape. Continue adding more petals, then trim the thick base. Leave to dry for 2 hours in a clean egg box lined with foil or clingfilm.

Making Lilies – Colour a little sugarpaste a deep yellow and mould this into thin sausage shapes. Leave these to firm on nonstick baking parchment or clingfilm for 2 hours. Thinly roll out white sugarpaste and mark out small squares of 4 x 4 cm/1 1/2 x 1 1/2 inches. Wrap each square round a yellow centre to form a lily and press the end together. Place the lilies on nonstick baking parchment to dry out for 2 hours.

Decorating Techniques

~ **Making Daisies** – Roll out a little sugarpaste thinly and, using a daisy stamp cutter, press out small flower shapes and mould these into a curve. Leave the daisies to dry out on nonstick baking parchment, then pipe dots into the centre of each one with yellow royal icing or a small gel tube of writing icing.

~ **Making Butterfly Wings** – Colour the sugarpaste and roll out thinly. Trace round the butterfly patterns on page 252 and cut out the wing shapes.

Leave these to dry flat on nonstick baking parchment for 4 hours to make them firm and easy to lift.

Decorating Tips

~ Always roll out almond paste or sugarpaste on a surface lightly dusted with icing sugar.

~ Leave sugarpaste-covered cakes to firm up for 2 hours before adding decorations, as this provides a good finished surface to work on.

~ Tie ribbons round the finished cake and secure them with a dab of royal icing. Never use pins in ribbons on a cake.

~ Once decorated, store sugarpaste-covered cakes in large boxes in a cool place. Do not store in the refrigerator, as the sugarpaste will become damp and colours may run.

~ Paste food colourings are best for working with sugarpaste, and a little goes a very long way. As these are very concentrated, use a cocktail stick to add dots of paste gradually, until you are sure of the colour, and knead in until even.

Everyday Icing

Recipes

Important as the baking is, the key component of any cupcake is surely the icing. This is where your imagination can really run riot! But it is a good idea to try out a few key icing recipes first. Here you will find icing recipes such as Basic Buttercream Frosting and Chocolate Fudge Icing, all of which can be applied to some of the other cupcake recipes in this book.

Cream Cheese Frosting

Covers 12 small cakes

50 g/2 oz unsalted butter, softened
at room temperature
300 g/11 oz icing sugar, sifted
flavouring of choice
food colourings of choice
125 g/4 oz full-fat cream cheese

Beat the butter and icing sugar together until light and fluffy.

Add flavourings and colourings of your choice and beat again.

Add the cream cheese and whisk until light and fluffy.

Do not overbeat, however, as the mixture can become runny.

Royal Icing

Makes 500 g/1 lb 1 oz to cover 12 deep cakes

2 medium egg whites
500 g/1 lb 1 oz icing sugar, sifted
2 tsp lemon juice

Put the egg whites in a large bowl and whisk lightly with a fork to break up the whites until foamy.

Sift in half the icing sugar with the lemon juice and beat well with an electric mixer for 4 minutes, or by hand with a wooden spoon for about 10 minutes, until smooth.

Gradually sift in the remaining icing sugar and beat again until thick, smooth and brilliant white and the icing forms soft peaks when flicked up with a spoon.

Keep the royal icing covered with a clean, damp cloth until ready for use, or store in the refrigerator in a plastic container until needed.

If making royal icing to use later, beat it again before use to remove any air bubbles that may have formed in the mixture.

Chocolate Fudge Icing

Covers 12 small cakes

125 g/4 oz dark chocolate,
broken into pieces
50 g/2 oz unsalted butter
1 medium egg, beaten
175 g/6 oz natural icing
sugar, sifted
$^1/_2$ tsp vanilla extract

Place the chocolate and butter in a bowl over a pan of hot water and stir until melted.

Remove from the heat and whisk in the egg with the icing sugar and vanilla extract.

Whisk until smooth and glossy, then use immediately or leave to cool and thicken for a spreading consistency.

Glacé Icing

Covers 12 small cakes

225 g/8 oz icing sugar
few drops lemon juice or vanilla or
almond extract
2–3 tbsp boiling water
liquid food colouring (optional)

Sift the icing sugar into a bowl and add the chosen flavouring.

Gradually stir in enough water to mix to the consistency of thick cream. Beat with a wooden spoon until the icing is thick enough to coat the back of the spoon.

Add colouring, if liked, and use at once, as the icing will begin to form a skin.

Variations

Chocolate Sift 2 tsp cocoa powder into the icing sugar.

Coffee Dissolve 1 tsp coffee granules in 1 tbsp of the hot water and cool or add 1 tsp liquid coffee extract.

Basic Buttercream

Covers 12 small cakes

150 g/5 oz unsalted butter,
softened at room temperature
225 g/8 oz icing sugar, sifted
2 tbsp hot milk or water
1 tsp vanilla extract
food colourings of choice

Beat the butter until light and fluffy, then beat in the
sifted icing sugar and hot milk or water in two batches.

Add the vanilla extract and any colourings. Store
chilled for up to 2 days in a lidded container.

Variations

Omit the vanilla extract and instead:

Coffee Blend 2 tsp coffee extract with the milk.

Chocolate Blend 2 tbsp cocoa powder to a
paste with 2 tbsp boiling water and use instead
of the hot milk or water.

Almond Paste

Makes 450 g/1 lb to cover
24 small cakes

125 g/4 oz sifted icing sugar
125 g/4 oz caster sugar
225 g/8 oz ground almonds
1 medium egg
1 tsp lemon juice

Stir the sugars and ground almonds together in a bowl.

Whisk the egg and lemon juice together and mix into the dry ingredients.

Knead until the paste is smooth. Wrap tightly in clingfilm or foil to keep airtight and store in the refrigerator until needed.

The paste can be made 2–3 days ahead of time but, after that, it will start to dry out and become difficult to handle.

To use the paste, knead on a surface dusted with icing sugar. Brush the top of each cake with apricot glaze.

Roll out the almond paste and cut out discs large enough to cover the tops of the cakes. Press onto the cakes.

Apricot Glaze

Makes 450 g/1 lb to cover 24 small cakes

450 g/1 lb apricot jam
3 tbsp water
1 tsp lemon juice

Place the jam, water and juice in a heavy-based saucepan and heat gently, stirring, until soft and melted.

Boil rapidly for 1 minute, then press through a fine sieve with the back of a wooden spoon. Discard the pieces of fruit.

Use immediately for glazing or sticking on almond paste, or pour into a clean jar or plastic lidded container and store in the refrigerator for up to 3 months.

Sugarpaste

**Makes 350 g/12 oz to cover
12 small cakes or use
for decorations**

1 medium egg white
1 tbsp liquid glucose
350 g/12 oz icing sugar, sifted

Place the egg white and liquid glucose in a large mixing bowl and stir together, breaking up the egg white.

Add the icing sugar gradually, mixing in until the mixture binds together and forms a ball.

Turn the ball of icing out onto a clean surface dusted with icing sugar and knead for 5 minutes until soft but firm enough to roll out.

If the icing is too soft, knead in a little more icing sugar until the mixture is pliable.

To colour, knead in paste food colouring. Do not use liquid food colouring, as this is not suitable and will make the sugarpaste limp.

To use, roll out thinly on a clean surface dusted with icing sugar and cut out discs large enough to cover the top of each cake.

Teatime

Cupcakes

Effortlessly dainty and timelessly classic, cupcakes are the perfect teatime treat for any day. Old favourites such as Lemon Drizzle Cupcakes or Madeleine Cupcakes, as well as elegant recipes such as Fondant Fancies, will delight any sweet tooth. These treats use a range of decorating and icing techniques, and all of them make a mouthwatering accompaniment to a comforting cup of tea.

Basic Vanilla Cupcakes

Makes 18 deep cupcakes or 24 fairy cakes

225 g/8 oz butter, softened
at room temperature
225 g/8 oz caster sugar
4 medium eggs, beaten
225 g/8 oz self-raising flour
$1/2$ tsp baking powder
2 tbsp semi-skimmed milk
1 tsp vanilla extract
1 tsp glycerine

Preheat the oven to 180°C/350°F/Gas Mark 4 and line appropriate trays with enough paper cases.

Whisk the butter and sugar together, preferably with an electric hand-mixer, until pale and fluffy. Whisk in the egg, gradually, adding a teaspoon of flour with each addition to prevent the mixture from curdling.

Sift the remaining flour and the baking powder into the bowl, then gradually whisk in the milk, vanilla extract and glycerine. Spoon the mixture into the paper cases and bake for 25 minutes for the larger cakes, 15 minutes for the fairy cakes, or until firm and golden. Cool on a wire rack. Keep for 3–4 days in an airtight container.

Mini Carrot Cupcakes

Makes 22

175 g/6 oz self-raising
wholemeal flour
1 tsp baking powder
$^1/_2$ tsp ground cinnamon
pinch salt
150 ml/$^1/_4$ pint sunflower oil
150 g/5 oz soft light
brown sugar
3 medium eggs, beaten
1 tsp vanilla extract
50 g/2 oz sultanas
225 g/8 oz carrots, peeled
and grated

To decorate

1 orange
75 g/3 oz cream cheese
175 g/6 oz golden icing sugar

Preheat the oven to 180°C/350°F/Gas Mark 4. Lightly oil two 12-hole mini trays.

Sift the flour, baking powder, cinnamon and salt into a bowl, along with any bran from the sieve. Add the oil, sugar, eggs, vanilla extract, sultanas and grated carrots.

Beat until smooth, then spoon into the trays. Bake for about 20 minutes until risen and golden. Cool on a wire rack.

To decorate, peel thin strips of zest from the orange. Beat the cream cheese and icing sugar together with 2 teaspoons juice from the orange to make a spreading consistency. Swirl the icing over each cupcake and then top with shreds of orange zest. Keep for 3 days in an airtight container in a cool place.

Double Cherry Cupcakes

Makes 12 large cupcakes or 18 fairy cakes

50 g/2 oz glacé cherries, washed, dried and chopped
125 g/4 oz self-raising flour
25 g/1 oz dried morello cherries
125 g/4 oz soft margarine
125 g/4 oz caster sugar
2 medium eggs
$1/2$ tsp almond extract

To decorate

125 g/4 oz fondant icing sugar
pale pink liquid food colouring
40 g/$1^1/2$ oz glacé cherries

Preheat the oven to 190°C/375°F/Gas Mark 5. Line a 12-hole tray with deep paper cases, or two trays with 18 fairy-cake cases.

Dust the chopped glacé cherries lightly in a tablespoon of the flour, then mix with the morello cherries and set aside. Sift the rest of the flour into a bowl, then add the margarine, sugar, eggs and almond extract. Beat for about 2 minutes until smooth, then fold in the cherries.

Spoon the batter into the paper cases and bake for 15–20 minutes until well risen and springy in the centre. Turn out to cool on a wire rack.

To decorate the cupcakes, trim the tops level. Mix the icing sugar with 2–3 teaspoons warm water and a few drops of pink food colouring to make a thick consistency. Spoon the icing over each cupcake filling right up to the edge. Chop the cherries finely and sprinkle over the icing. Leave to set for 30 minutes. Keep for 3 days in an airtight container.

Lemon Drizzle Cupcakes

Makes 12 deep cupcakes or 18 fairy cakes

150 g/5 oz butter, softened
150 g/5 oz caster sugar
3 medium eggs, beaten
150 g/5 oz self-raising flour
$^1/_2$ tsp baking powder
1 lemon

To decorate

1 lemon
50 g/2 oz caster sugar

Preheat the oven to 180°C/350°F/Gas Mark 4 and line a 12-hole tray with paper cases, or two fairy-cake trays with 18 fairy-cake cases.

Place the butter, sugar and eggs in a bowl and then sift in the flour and baking powder. Finely grate the zest of the lemon into the bowl.

Beat together for about 2 minutes, preferably with an electric hand-mixer, until pale and fluffy. Spoon into the paper cases and bake for 25 minutes for the larger cupcakes and 15 minutes for the fairy cakes until firm and golden. Cool on a wire rack.

To make the topping, cut the zest from the other lemon into thin strips and set aside. Squeeze the juice from the lemon into a small saucepan. Add the sugar and heat gently until every grain of sugar has dissolved.

Add the strips of zest and cool slightly. Spoon the syrup and lemon strips over the cupcakes while still warm. Leave to cool. Keep for 4 days in an airtight container.

Cream Cheese Pastel Swirls

Makes 12

150 g/5 oz butter, softened
150 g/5 oz caster sugar
175 g/6 oz self-raising flour
3 medium eggs
1 tsp vanilla extract

To decorate

1 batch cream cheese frosting
(see page 52)
paste food colourings

Preheat the oven to 180°C/350°F/Gas Mark 4. Line a 12-hole tray with deep paper cases.

Place the butter and sugar in a bowl and cream together. In another bowl, beat the eggs with the vanilla extract. Sift the flour into the creamed mixture, then beat in the eggs until smooth. Spoon into the cases, filling them three-quarters full.

Bake for about 18 minutes until firm to the touch in the centre. Turn out to cool on a wire rack.

Divide the frosting into three batches. Colour one green and one pink with dots of food colouring and leave one batch plain. Place each batch in a piping bag fitted with a star nozzle and pipe large swirls on top of each cupcake. Keep for 3 days in an airtight container in a cool place.

Fondant Fancies

Makes 16–18

150 g/5 oz self-raising flour
150 g/5 oz caster sugar
50 g/2 oz ground almonds
150 g/5 oz butter, softened
3 medium eggs, beaten
4 tbsp milk

To decorate

450 g/1 lb fondant icing sugar
paste food colourings
selection fancy cake decorations

Preheat the oven to 180˚C/350˚F/Gas Mark 4. Line two 12-hole bun trays with 16–18 paper cases, depending on the depth of the holes.

Sift the flour into a bowl and stir in the caster sugar and almonds. Add the butter, eggs and milk and beat until smooth.

Spoon into the paper cases and bake for 15–20 minutes until golden and firm to the touch. Turn out to cool on a wire rack. When cool, trim the tops flat if they have peaked slightly.

To decorate the cupcakes, make the fondant icing to a thick coating consistency, following the packet instructions. Divide into batches and colour each separately with a little paste food colouring. Keep each bowl covered with a damp cloth until needed. Spoon some icing over each cupcake, being sure to flood it right to the edge. Top each with a fancy decoration and leave to set for 30 minutes. Keep for 2 days in a cool place.

Madeleine Cupcakes

Makes 10–12

125 g/4 oz self-raising flour
125 g/4 oz butter, softened
125 g/4 oz golden caster sugar
2 medium eggs, beaten
1 tsp vanilla extract

To decorate

4 tbsp seedless raspberry jam
65 g/2$\frac{1}{2}$ oz desiccated coconut
glacé cherries, halved

Preheat the oven to 180°C/350°F/Gas Mark 4. Line a 12-hole tray with 10–12 paper cases, depending on the depth of the holes.

Sift the flour into a bowl and add the butter, sugar, eggs and vanilla extract. Beat for about 2 minutes until smooth, then spoon into the paper cases.

Bake in the centre of the oven for about 14–16 minutes until well risen and springy in the centre. Transfer to a wire rack to cool.

To decorate the cupcakes, warm the raspberry jam in a small pan or in the microwave oven in a heatproof dish on low for a few seconds. Brush the warmed jam over the top of each cupcake. Lightly coat the top of each cupcake with coconut, then finish with a halved cherry. Keep for 3 days in an airtight container.

Strawberry Swirl Cupcakes

Makes 12

125 g/4 oz caster sugar
125 g/4 oz soft tub margarine
2 medium eggs
125 g/4 oz self-raising flour
$^1/_2$ tsp baking powder
2 tbsp sieved strawberry jam

To decorate

50 g/2 oz unsalted butter at room
temperature
300 g/11 oz icing
sugar, sifted
125 g/4 oz full-fat
cream cheese
1 tbsp sieved strawberry jam
pink food colouring

Preheat the oven to 190°C/375°F/Gas Mark 5. Line a tray with 12 deep paper cases.

Place all the cupcake ingredients except the jam in a large bowl and beat with an electric mixer for about 2 minutes until smooth. Fill the paper cases halfway up with the mixture.

Add $^1/_2$ teaspoon jam to each case and swirl it into the mixture. Bake for about 15 minutes until firm, risen and golden. Remove to a wire rack to cool.

To prepare the frosting, beat the butter until soft, then gradually add the icing sugar until the mixture is light. Add the cream cheese and whisk until light and fluffy. Divide the mixture in half and beat the strawberry jam and pink food colouring into one half. Fit a piping bag with a wide star nozzle and spoon strawberry cream on one side of the bag and the plain cream on the other. Pipe swirls on top of the cupcakes. Keep for 3 days in an airtight container in a cool place.

Rose Petal Cupcakes

Makes 12

125 g/4 oz self-raising flour
125 g/4 oz butter, softened
125 g/4 oz golden
caster sugar
2 medium eggs, beaten
1 tbsp rosewater

To decorate

1 egg white
about 80 small, dry
rose petals
caster sugar, for dusting
175 g/6 oz icing sugar
1 tbsp glycerine
2 tbsp rosewater
pink food colouring

Preheat the oven to 180°C/350°F/Gas Mark 4. Line a 12-hole bun tray with foil cases.

Sift the flour into a bowl and add the butter, sugar, eggs and rosewater. Beat for about 2 minutes until smooth, then spoon into the cases.

Bake in the centre of the oven for about 14 minutes until well risen and springy in the centre. Transfer to a wire rack to cool. Keep undecorated for up to 2 days in an airtight container.

To decorate, first place a large piece of nonstick baking parchment on a flat surface. Beat the egg white until frothy, then brush thinly over the rose petals. Set the petals on the paper. Dust with caster sugar and leave for 3 hours until dry and sparkling.

Beat the icing sugar with the glycerine and rosewater and add enough colouring to give a pale pink colour. Spread over the top of each cupcake and add a circle of rose petals, working quickly, as the icing will begin to set. Leave for 30 minutes before serving. Eat on the day of decorating.

Almond ❧ Cherry Cupcakes

Makes 12

50 g/2 oz glacé cherries, plus
extra for decoration
125 g/4 oz self-raising flour, plus
extra for dusting
125 g/4 oz soft margarine
125 g/4 oz caster sugar
2 medium eggs
$\frac{1}{2}$ tsp almond extract

To decorate

125 g/4 oz icing sugar
1 tsp lemon juice
pink food colouring

Preheat the oven to 190°C/375°F/Gas Mark 5. Line a 12-hole bun tray with small paper cases. Wash the glacé cherries, then dry them thoroughly. Chop the cherries, then dust lightly in flour and set aside.

Sift the flour into a bowl, then add the margarine, sugar, eggs and almond extract. Beat until smooth for about 2 minutes, then fold in the chopped cherries.

Spoon into the paper cases. Bake for 15–20 minutes until golden and springy in the centre. Turn out to cool on a wire rack.

To decorate, mix the icing sugar with the lemon juice and 2 teaspoons water to form a smooth glacé icing. Add a little pink food colouring and drizzle over the top of each cupcake. Place a halved cherry on top and leave to set for 30 minutes. Keep for 2–3 days in an airtight container.

Quilted Cupcakes

ℭ

Makes 12–14

125 g/4 oz self-raising flour
125 g/4 oz caster sugar
125 g/4 oz soft margarine
2 medium eggs, beaten
1 tsp lemon juice

To decorate

125 g/4 oz buttercream
(see page 60)
450 g/1 lb ready-to-roll sugarpaste
edible gold or silver balls

Preheat the oven to 180°C/350°F/Gas Mark 4. Line two 12-hole bun trays with 12–14 foil cases, depending on the depth of the holes.

Sift the flour into a bowl and stir together with the caster sugar. Add the margarine and eggs and beat together with the lemon juice for about 2 minutes until smooth.

Spoon into the cases and bake for 15–20 minutes until golden and firm to the touch. Turn out on a wire rack. When cool, trim the tops flat if they have peaked slightly.

To decorate, lightly coat the top of each cupcake with a little buttercream. Dust a clean, flat surface with icing sugar. Roll out the sugarpaste and stamp out circles 6 cm/2^1/$_2$ inches wide. Place these on the buttercream to cover the top of each cupcake. Take a palette knife and press lines into the icing, then mark across in the opposite direction to make small squares. Place an edible gold or silver ball into the corner of each square. Keep for 3 days in an airtight container in a cool place.

Daisy Chain Lemon Cupcakes

Makes 12

125 g/4 oz caster sugar
125 g/4 oz soft tub margarine
2 medium eggs
125 g/4 oz self-raising flour
1/2 tsp baking powder
1 tsp lemon juice

To decorate

50 g/2 oz ready-to-roll
sugarpaste icing
yellow piping icing tube
225 g/8 oz fondant
icing sugar
lemon yellow food colouring

Preheat the oven to 190°C/375°F/Gas Mark 5. Line a bun tray with 12 paper cases.

Place all the cupcake ingredients in a large bowl and beat with an electric mixer for about 2 minutes until smooth. Fill the paper cases halfway up with the mixture.

Bake for about 15 minutes until firm, risen and golden. Remove to a wire rack to cool.

Roll out the icing thinly and stamp out small daisies with a fluted daisy cutter. Pipe a small yellow dot of icing into the centre of each and leave to dry out for 1 hour. Blend the fondant icing sugar with a little water and a few dots of yellow colouring to make a thick, easy-to-spread icing, then smooth over the top of each cupcake. Decorate with the cut-out daisies immediately and leave to set for 1 hour. Keep for 3 days in an airtight container.

Chocolate

Cupcakes

Cupcakes offer limitless ways to experiment with chocolate and allow indulgent exploration for any chocoholic. Orange Drizzle Chocolate Cupcakes have a light and fruity contrast, while the Chocolate Fudge Flake Cupcakes are pure chocolate decadence. To add a sophisticated edge, try the Mocha Cupcakes or White Chocolate Cupcakes, perfect for sharing, if you can bear to give any away!

Double Chocolate Chip Cupcakes

Makes 14

125 g/4 oz soft margarine
125 g/4 oz golden caster sugar
2 medium eggs, beaten
25 g/1 oz cocoa powder
175 g/6 oz self-raising flour
1 tsp baking powder
50 g/2 oz milk chocolate chips
50 g/2 oz dark or white
chocolate chips
1 tbsp milk

Preheat the oven to 180°C/350°F/Gas Mark 4. Line one or two bun trays with 14 small paper cases.

Place the margarine and sugar in a large bowl with the eggs and sift in the cocoa powder, flour and baking powder. Beat for about 2 minutes until smooth, then fold in the chocolate chips with the milk.

Spoon into the paper cases and bake for 15–20 minutes until firm. Place on a wire rack to cool. Keep for 4–5 days in an airtight container.

White Chocolate Cupcakes

Makes 12

200 g/7 oz butter
125 g/4 oz white chocolate
50 g/2 oz plain flour
200 g/7 oz self-raising flour
1 tsp baking powder
200 g/7 oz caster sugar
finely grated zest of $1/2$ lemon
3 medium eggs
100 ml/$3^1/2$ fl oz natural yogurt
250 g/9 oz white chocolate,
to decorate

Preheat the oven to 180°C/350°F/Gas Mark 4. Line a deep 12-hole tray with paper cases. Melt the butter and leave aside to cool.

Coarsely grate or chop the white chocolate. Sift the flours and baking powder into a bowl and stir in the sugar, lemon zest and chopped white chocolate. In another bowl, whisk together the eggs and yogurt. Pour into the dry ingredients with the cooled melted butter and beat until combined. Spoon into the paper cases and bake for 25 minutes until firm and golden.

To decorate the cupcakes, melt one quarter of the white chocolate in a heatproof bowl standing over a pan of barely simmering water. Spread the melted chocolate out onto a clean plastic board. When almost set, make into curls by pulling a sharp knife through the chocolate. Refrigerate for 30 minutes to set.

Melt the remaining white chocolate, then spoon over the cupcakes and leave for about 10 minutes until cooled and half set. Top each cupcake while still wet with the white chocolate curls and leave to set for 30 minutes. Keep for 2 days in the refrigerator.

Chocolate Fudge Flake Cupcakes

Makes 12 large cupcakes
or 18 fairy cakes

125 g/4 oz self-raising flour
25 g/1 oz cocoa powder
125 g/4 oz soft margarine
125 g/4 oz soft light
brown sugar
2 medium eggs, beaten
2 tbsp milk

To decorate

25 g/1 oz butter
50 g/2 oz golden syrup
15 g/$\frac{1}{2}$ oz cocoa powder
125 g/4 oz golden icing sugar
25 g/1 oz cream cheese
40 g/1$\frac{1}{2}$ oz chocolate flake bar

Preheat the oven to 180°C/350°F/Gas Mark 4. Line a 12-hole tray with deep paper cases, or one or two trays with 18 fairy-cake cases.

Sift the flour and cocoa powder into a large bowl, add the margarine, sugar, eggs and milk and whisk with an electric beater for about 2 minutes until smooth.

Divide the mixture between the paper cases and bake for about 20 minutes for the larger cupcakes and 15 minutes for the fairy cakes until a skewer inserted into the middle comes out clean. Turn out to cool on a wire rack.

To make the topping, melt the butter with the syrup and cocoa powder in a pan. Cool, then whisk in the icing sugar until the mixture has thickened, and beat in the cream cheese. Spread the frosting over the cupcakes. Chop the flake bar into small chunks, then place one chunk in the centre of each cupcake. Keep for 2–3 days in the refrigerator.

Black Forest Cupcakes

Makes 12 large cupcakes or 24 small cupcakes

1 tbsp cocoa powder
2 tbsp boiling water
175 g/6 oz self-raising flour
1 tsp baking powder
125 g/4 oz soft tub margarine
175 g/6 oz soft dark brown sugar
2 medium eggs
3 tbsp milk

To decorate

125 g/4 oz dark chocolate
4 tbsp seedless raspberry jam, warmed
150 ml/¼ pint double cream
1 tbsp Kirsch (optional)
12 natural-coloured glacé cherries

Preheat the oven to 180°C/350°F/Gas Mark 4. Line a 12-hole tray with large paper cases, or one or two bun trays with 24 small paper cases. Blend the cocoa powder with the boiling water and leave to cool.

Sift the flour and baking powder into a bowl and add the margarine, sugar, eggs, milk and the cocoa mixture. Whisk together for about 2 minutes until smooth, then spoon into the paper cases.

Bake for 15–20 minutes until springy to the touch. Cool in the tins for 5 minutes, then turn out onto a wire rack to cool.

To decorate the cupcakes, melt the chocolate and spread it out to cool on a clean plastic board. When it is almost set, pull a sharp knife through the chocolate to make curls. Refrigerate these until needed. Brush the top of each cupcake with a little raspberry jam. Whisk the cream until it forms soft peaks, then fold in the kirsch, if using. Pipe or swirl the cream on top of each cupcake. Top with chocolate curls and whole glacé cherries for the large cakes or halved cherries for the smaller ones. Eat fresh or keep for 1 day in the refrigerator.

Sticky Toffee Cupcakes

Makes 16–18

150 g/5 oz stoned dates, chopped
1 tsp bicarbonate of soda
225 ml/8 fl oz hot water
175 g/6 oz plain flour
1 tsp baking powder
50 g/2 oz butter or block
margarine, diced
200 g/7 oz soft light
brown sugar
1 large egg, beaten
$\frac{1}{2}$ tsp vanilla extract

For the icing

25 g/1 oz unsalted butter
5 tbsp soft light brown sugar
4 tbsp double cream

Preheat the oven to 180°C/350°F/Gas Mark 4. Line one or two bun trays with 16–18 fairy-cake cases, depending on the depth of the holes. Place the chopped dates in a bowl with the bicarbonate of soda and pour over the hot water. Stir, then set aside to cool.

Sift the flour and baking powder into a bowl and add the diced butter. Rub in between your fingertips until the mixture resembles fine crumbs. Stir in the sugar and mix well. Add the egg, vanilla extract and the date mixture. Beat with a wooden spoon until smooth.

Spoon into the cases and bake for about 25 minutes until well risen and firm to the touch in the centre. Leave to cool in the tray for 5 minutes, then turn out to cool on a wire rack.

To make the topping, place the butter, sugar and cream in a small pan over a low heat and stir until the sugar dissolves. Bring to the boil and boil for 1–2 minutes until the mixture thickens. Brush quickly over each cake, as the mixture will set as it cools. Keep for 2 days in an airtight container.

Mocha Cupcakes

c

Makes 12

125 g/4 oz soft margarine
125 g/4 oz golden caster sugar
150 g/5 oz self-raising flour
2 tbsp cocoa powder
2 medium eggs
1 tbsp golden syrup
2 tbsp milk

To decorate

225 g/8 oz golden icing sugar
125 g/4 oz unsalted
butter, softened
2 tsp coffee extract
12 cape gooseberries, papery
covering pulled back

Preheat the oven to 180°C/350°F/Gas Mark 4. Line a 12-hole tray with deep paper cases.

Place the margarine and sugar in a large bowl, then sift in the flour and cocoa powder.

In another bowl, beat the eggs with the syrup, then add to the cocoa mixture. Whisk everything together with the milk using an electric beater for 2 minutes, or by hand with a wooden spoon.

Divide the mixture between the cases, filling them three-quarters full. Bake for about 20 minutes until the centres are springy to the touch. Turn out to cool on a wire rack.

Make the frosting by sifting the icing sugar into a bowl. Add the butter, coffee extract and 1 tablespoon hot water. Beat until fluffy, then swirl onto each cupcake with a flat-bladed knife. Top each with a fresh cape gooseberry. Keep for 2 days in a cool place.

Rocky Road Cupcakes

Makes 14–18

125 g/4 oz self-raising flour
25 g/1 oz cocoa powder
125 g/4 oz soft dark
brown sugar
125 g/4 oz soft margarine
2 medium eggs, beaten
2 tbsp milk

To decorate

75 g/3 oz dark chocolate, broken
into squares
40 g/1½ oz butter
75 g/3 oz mini marshmallows
40 g/1½ oz chopped
mixed nuts

Preheat the oven to 180°C/350°F/Gas Mark 4. Line bun trays with 14–18 paper cases or silicone cupcake moulds, depending on the depth of the holes.

Sift the flour and cocoa powder into a large bowl. Add the sugar, margarine, eggs and milk and whisk with an electric beater for about 2 minutes until smooth.

Divide the mixture evenly between the paper cases and bake for about 20 minutes until a skewer inserted into the middle comes out clean. Remove the tray from the oven but leave the oven on.

To make the topping, gently melt the chocolate and butter together in a small pan over a low heat. Place the melted chocolate mixture in an icing bag made of greaseproof paper and snip away the end. Pipe a little of the mixture on top of each cupcake, then scatter the marshmallows and nuts over each one and return to the oven. Bake for 2–3 minutes to soften the marshmallows. Remove from the oven and pipe the remaining chocolate over the marshmallows. Leave to cool in the trays for 5 minutes, then remove to cool on a wire rack. Serve warm or cold. Keep for 2 days in an airtight container.

Chocolate ❦ Toffee Cupcakes

Makes 12–14

125 g/4 oz soft fudge
125 g/4 oz soft margarine
125 g/4 oz golden
caster sugar
150 g/5 oz self-raising flour
2 tbsp cocoa powder
2 medium eggs
1 tbsp golden syrup
1 batch cream cheese frosting
(see page 52),
to decorate

Preheat the oven to 180°C/350°F/Gas Mark 4. Line one or two bun trays with 12–14 paper cases, depending on the depth of the holes. Cut one quarter of the fudge into slices for decoration. Chop the rest into small cubes. Set all the fudge aside.

Place the margarine and the sugar in a large bowl and then sift in the flour and cocoa powder. In another bowl, beat the eggs with the syrup, then add to the flour mixture. Whisk together with an electric beater for 2 minutes, or by hand with a wooden spoon until smooth. Gently fold in the fudge cubes.

Spoon the mixture into the cases, filling them three-quarters full. Bake for about 15 minutes until a skewer inserted into the centre comes out clean. Turn out to cool on a wire rack.

Swirl the cream cheese frosting over each cupcake, then finish by topping with a fudge slice. Keep for 3–4 days chilled in a sealed container.

Very Rich Chocolate Cupcakes

Makes 12–14

75 g/3 oz self-raising flour
25 g/1 oz cocoa powder
75 g/3 oz soft dark
brown sugar
75 g/3 oz butter, softened
3 medium eggs
2 tbsp milk

To decorate

200 g/7 oz dark chocolate
100 ml/3½ fl oz whipping cream
1 tbsp liquid glucose
selection chocolate decorations

Preheat the oven to 190°C/375°F/Gas Mark 5. Line one or two 12-hole bun trays with 12–14 paper cases, depending on the depth of the holes.

Sift the flour and cocoa powder into a bowl and add the sugar, butter, eggs and milk. Whisk until smooth, then spoon into the paper cases.

Bake for about 14 minutes until just firm to the touch in the centre. Transfer to a wire rack to cool.

To decorate the cupcakes, break the chocolate into pieces and melt in a heatproof bowl standing over a pan of warm water. In another pan, bring the cream to just below boiling, then remove from the heat and stir in the liquid glucose. Add the melted chocolate and stir until smooth and glossy. Spoon over the cupcakes and immediately top each with a chocolate decoration. Leave to set for 30 minutes. Keep for 3 days in an airtight container in a cool place.

Unbaked Chocolate Cupcakes

Makes 8

For the cases

450 g/1 lb dark chocolate

For the filling

50 g/2 oz trifle sponges
2 tbsp sweet sherry or
orange liqueur
350 g/12 oz strawberries
450 ml/³/₄ pint double cream

Wash eight ridged, deep silicone moulds and dry them with kitchen paper to ensure they are completely free of moisture. Break the chocolate into small pieces and place in a bowl. Set the bowl over a saucepan of warm water and heat the water to barely simmering to melt the chocolate, or place the bowl in the microwave and melt on low in bursts of 30 seconds.

When the chocolate has melted, brush it round the insides of the moulds with a teaspoon or pastry brush, making sure to go into all the ridges. Chill the moulds for 1 hour. When the chocolate has set, brush on another, thicker layer inside the cases and chill again. Once the cases are solid, carefully peel the silicone moulds away from the outsides.

Cut a cube of trifle sponge to fit inside a chocolate case, put inside the case and sprinkle the sponge with sherry or liqueur. Place a small or halved strawberry on top of this. Repeat with the remaining chocolate cases. Whip the cream until it forms soft peaks and place in a piping bag fitted with a large star nozzle. Pipe swirls into each case and top with another small or halved strawberry. Refrigerate until needed for up to 24 hours.

Orange Drizzle Cupcakes

Makes 10

75 g/3 oz dark
chocolate, chopped
125 g/4 oz butter
125 g/4 oz caster sugar
2 medium eggs, beaten
200 g/7 oz self-raising flour
zest of 1/2 orange,
finely grated
5 tbsp thick natural yogurt

To decorate

1 batch orange-flavoured
buttercream (see page 60)
2 tbsp marmalade

Preheat the oven to 190°C/375°F/Gas Mark 5. Grease 10 deep moulds or line a 12-hole tray with 10 deep paper cases.

Melt the chocolate in a heatproof bowl over a pan of warm water or in the microwave oven on low for 30 seconds and leave to cool.

Put the butter and sugar in a large bowl and whisk until light and fluffy. Gradually beat in the eggs, adding a teaspoon of flour with each addition. Beat in the cooled melted chocolate, then sift in the flour. Add the orange zest and yogurt to the bowl and whisk until smooth.

Spoon the mixture into the paper cases and bake for about 25 minutes until well risen and springy to the touch. Leave for 2 minutes in the moulds or tray, then turn out onto a wire rack.

To decorate, fill a piping bag fitted with a star nozzle with the buttercream and pipe swirls on top of each cupcake. Warm the marmalade and drizzle around the sides of the cupcakes with a teaspoon. Keep in an airtight container in a cool place for 4 days.

Blondie Cupcakes

Makes 14 large cupcakes or 24 mini cupcakes

175 g/6 oz unsalted butter, softened
300 g/11 oz caster sugar
3 medium eggs, beaten
1 tsp vanilla extract
200 g/7 oz plain flour
1 tsp baking powder
100 g/3^1/$_2$ oz white chocolate chips
90 g/3^1/$_4$ oz pecan nuts, roughly chopped
90 g/3^1/$_4$ oz ready-to-eat dried apricots, roughly chopped
1 tbsp milk
50 g/2 oz white chocolate, melted, to decorate

Preheat the oven to 180°C/350°F/Gas Mark 4. Line two trays with 14 deep paper cases, or one mini tray with 24 paper cases.

Beat the butter with the sugar until light and fluffy, then add the eggs and vanilla extract gradually, beating between each addition. Sift the flour and baking powder into the bowl, then fold the white chocolate chips, nuts and apricots into the mixture along with the milk until evenly combined.

Spoon the mixture into the prepared trays. Bake for about 25 minutes until just firm. Leave in the tray(s) for 10 minutes, then turn out to cool on a wire rack.

Fill a small, greaseproof paper icing bag with the melted chocolate and snip away the end. Pipe a drizzle pattern on top of the cupcakes and leave to set for 30 minutes. Keep in an airtight container for 5 days.

Chocolate Mud Cupcakes

Makes 16

150 g/5 oz butter, softened
150 g/5 oz golden caster sugar
3 medium eggs, beaten
125 g/4 oz self-raising flour
25 g/1 oz cocoa powder

To decorate

75 g/3 oz milk chocolate
75 g/3 oz unsalted butter, softened
150 g/5 oz golden icing
sugar, sifted
white and dark chocolate sprinkles

Preheat the oven to 190°C/375°F/Gas Mark 5. Line one or two bun trays with 16 foil or paper cases.

Place the butter, caster sugar and eggs in a large bowl and then sift in the flour and cocoa powder. Whisk together for about 2 minutes until smooth, then spoon into the cases, filling them two-thirds full.

Bake for about 14 minutes until well risen and springy to the touch. Cool on a wire rack.

To make the frosting, break the chocolate into squares and melt in a heatproof bowl over a pan of barely simmering water. Set aside to cool. Beat the butter and icing sugar together until fluffy, then whisk in the cooled melted chocolate. Swirl over the cupcakes with a flat-bladed knife. Scatter over the sprinkles. Keep for 3 days in a cool place.

Mint Choc Chip Cupcakes

Makes 12

125 g/4 oz soft margarine
125 g/4 oz golden
caster sugar
2 medium eggs
175 g/6 oz self-raising flour
25 g/1 oz cocoa powder
1 tsp baking powder
75 g/3 oz dark
chocolate chips
25 g/1 oz clear, hard peppermint
sweets, crushed into crumbs

To decorate

50 g/2 oz unsalted butter
175 g/6 oz icing sugar
peppermint flavouring
or extract
green food colouring
50 g/2 oz chocolate squares

Preheat the oven to 180°C/350°F/Gas Mark 4. Line a 12-hole tray with deep paper cases.

Place the margarine, sugar and eggs in a bowl, then sift in the flour, cocoa powder and baking powder. Beat by hand or with an electric mixer until smooth, then fold in the chocolate chips and the crushed mints.

Spoon the mixture into the paper cases and bake for 15–20 minutes until firm in the centre. Remove to a wire rack to cool.

Beat the butter and icing sugar together with 1 tablespoon warm water, the peppermint flavouring or extract and the food colouring. Place in a piping bag with a star nozzle and pipe swirls on top of each cupcake.

Cut the chocolate into triangles and place one on top of each cake. Keep for 3–4 days in an airtight container in a cool place.

Cupcakes for Entertaining

The seasoned cupcake lover will know that these lovely little cakes aren't just for kids! There are lots of options for entertaining, from Shaggy Coconut Cupcakes to Banoffee Cupcakes, and even Crystallised Violet Cupcakes to really impress your friends and family. These recipes would make a great dinner party dessert or party favour, and are sure to leave a lasting impression!

Ginger & Lemon Cupcakes

Makes 18

8 tbsp golden syrup
125 g/4 oz block margarine
225 g/8 oz plain flour
2 tsp ground ginger
75 g/3 oz sultanas
50 g/2 oz soft dark
brown sugar
200 ml/7 fl oz milk
1 tsp bicarbonate of soda
1 medium egg, beaten

To decorate

125 g/4 oz golden icing sugar
1 tsp lemon juice
glacé ginger pieces

Preheat the oven to 180°C/350°F/Gas Mark 4. Line two shallow trays with 18 paper cases.

Place the syrup and margarine in a heavy-based pan and melt together gently. Sift the flour and ginger into a bowl, then stir in the sultanas and sugar. Warm the milk and stir in the bicarbonate of soda.

Pour the syrup mixture, milk and beaten egg into the dry ingredients and beat until smooth. Pour the mixture into a jug.

Carefully spoon 2 tablespoons of the mixture into each case (the mixture will be wet). Bake for about 30 minutes. Cool in the trays for 10 minutes, then turn out to cool on a wire rack.

To decorate, blend the icing sugar with the lemon juice and 1 tablespoon warm water to make a thin glacé icing. Drizzle over the top of each cupcake, then top with glacé ginger pieces. Leave to set for 30 minutes. Keep in an airtight container for up to 5 days.

Coffee & Walnut Fudge Cupcakes

Makes 16–18

125 g/4 oz self-raising flour
125 g/4 oz butter, softened
125 g/4 oz golden
caster sugar
2 medium eggs, beaten
1 tbsp golden syrup
50 g/2 oz walnuts,
finely chopped

To decorate

225 g/8 oz golden icing sugar
125 g/4 oz unsalted butter, at room
temperature
2 tsp coffee extract
16–18 small walnut pieces

Preheat the oven to 200°C/400°F/Gas Mark 6. Line two 12-hole bun trays with 16–18 small foil cases, depending on the depth of the holes.

Stir the flour into a bowl and add the butter, sugar, eggs and syrup. Beat for about 2 minutes, then fold in the walnuts.

Spoon the mixture into the paper cases and bake for about 12–14 minutes until well risen and springy in the centre. Remove to a wire rack to cool.

Make the frosting by sifting the icing sugar into a bowl. Add the butter, coffee extract and 1 tablespoon hot water. Beat until light and fluffy, then place in a piping bag fitted with a star nozzle. Pipe a swirl on each cupcake and top with a walnut piece. Keep for 3–4 days in an airtight container in a cool place.

Florentine-topped Cupcakes

Makes 18

150 g/5 oz butter, softened
150 g/5 oz caster sugar
175 g/6 oz self-raising flour
3 medium eggs
1 tsp vanilla extract
75 g/3 oz glacé
cherries, chopped
50 g/2 oz angelica, chopped
50 g/2 oz candied peel, chopped
50 g/2 oz dried cranberries

To decorate

75 g/3 oz plain or milk
chocolate, melted
50 g/2 oz flaked almonds

Preheat the oven to 180°C/350°F/Gas Mark 4. Line two 12-hole trays with 18 paper cases.

Place the butter and sugar in a bowl, then sift in the flour. In another bowl, beat the eggs with the vanilla extract, then add to the first mixture and beat until smooth. Fold in half the cherries, angelica, peel and cranberries. Spoon into the cases, filling them three-quarters full.

Bake for about 18 minutes until firm to the touch in the centre. Turn out to cool on a wire rack.

Spoon a little melted chocolate on top of each cupcake, then scatter the remaining cherries, angelica, peel and cranberries and the almonds into the wet chocolate. Drizzle the remaining chocolate over the fruit topping with a teaspoon and leave to set for 30 minutes. Keep for 2 days in an airtight container.

Lemon & Cardamom Cupcakes

Makes 12

1 tsp cardamom pods
200 g/7 oz butter
50 g/2 oz plain flour
200 g/7 oz self-raising flour
1 tsp baking powder
200 g/7 oz caster sugar
zest of 1 lemon, finely grated
3 medium eggs
100 ml/3^1/$_2$ fl oz natural yogurt
4 tbsp lemon curd

To decorate

250 g/9 oz tub mascarpone
6 tbsp icing sugar
1 tsp lemon juice
lemon zest strips

Preheat the oven to 180°C/350°F/Gas Mark 4. Line a 12-hole tray with deep paper cases. Crush the cardamom pods and remove the outer cases. Melt the butter and leave aside to cool.

Sift the flours and baking powder into a bowl and stir in the crushed seeds, sugar and lemon zest. In another bowl, whisk together the eggs and yogurt. Pour into the dry ingredients with the cooled melted butter and beat until combined.

Divide half the mixture between the paper cases, put a teaspoon of lemon curd into each, then top with the remaining mixture. Bake for about 25 minutes until golden.

To make the topping, beat the mascarpone with the icing sugar and lemon juice. Swirl onto each cupcake and top with lemon strips. Eat fresh on the day of baking once decorated, or store, undecorated, in an airtight container for up to 2 days and add the topping just before serving.

Banoffee Cupcakes

Makes 10–12

175 g/6 oz soft, ripe bananas
125 g/4 oz soft margarine
75 g/3 oz golden caster sugar
1 tbsp milk
2 medium eggs
225 g/8 oz plain flour
1 tbsp baking powder
75 g/3 oz mini soft
fudge pieces

To decorate

125 g/4oz golden icing sugar
10–12 semi-dried
banana flakes

Preheat the oven to 180°C/350°F/Gas Mark 4. Line a 12-hole tray with 10–12 deep paper cases, depending on the depth of the holes.

Peel and mash the bananas in a large bowl, then add the margarine, sugar, milk and eggs. Sift in the flour and baking powder and beat together for about 2 minutes until smooth.

Fold in 50 g/2 oz of the fudge pieces and then spoon the mixture into the paper cases. Bake for about 20 minutes until golden and firm. Remove from the baking tray to a wire rack to cool.

For the decoration, blend the icing sugar with 3–4 teaspoons cold water to make a thin icing. Drizzle over the top of each cupcake and, while the icing is still wet, top with the remaining mini fudge pieces and the banana flakes. Leave to dry out for 30 minutes to set the icing. Keep in an airtight container for 3 days.

Goth Cupcakes

Makes 12–14

125 g/4 oz self-raising flour
125 g/4 oz caster sugar
125 g/4 oz soft margarine
2 medium eggs, beaten
1 tsp vanilla extract

To decorate

350 g/12 oz fondant icing
sugar, sifted
black and green paste
food colourings
edible silver balls and decorations

Preheat the oven to 180°C/350°F/Gas Mark 4. Line two 12-hole bun trays with 12–14 paper fairy-cake cases or silicone moulds, depending on the depth of the holes.

Sift the flour into a bowl and stir together with the caster sugar. Add the margarine, eggs and vanilla extract and beat together for about 2 minutes until smooth.

Spoon into the cases and bake for 15–20 minutes until golden and firm to the touch. Turn out on a wire rack. When cool, trim the tops flat if they have peaked slightly.

To decorate, blend the fondant icing sugar with enough water to make a coating consistency. Colour half the icing black and half green. Spread over the top of each cupcake and place the silver balls round the outer edges. Decorate with metallic cake shapes and dry for 30 minutes. Keep for 2 days in a cool place in an airtight container.

Blue Bow Cupcakes

Makes 12

150 g/5 oz butter, softened
150 g/5 oz caster sugar
175 g/6 oz self-raising flour
3 medium eggs
1 tsp vanilla extract

To decorate

1 batch cream cheese frosting
(see page 52)
blue paste food colouring
narrow blue ribbon
cocktail sticks

Preheat the oven to 180˚C/350˚F/Gas Mark 4. Line a 12-hole tray with deep paper cases.

Place the butter and sugar in a bowl, then sift in the flour. In another bowl, beat the eggs with the vanilla extract, then add to the bowl. Beat until smooth, then spoon into the cases, filling them three-quarters full.

Bake for about 18 minutes until firm to the touch in the centre. Turn out to cool on a wire rack.

To decorate the cupcakes, colour the frosting with a few dots of blue food colouring. Place in a piping bag fitted with a star nozzle and pipe large swirls on top of each cupcake. Make tiny bows from the narrow ribbon and slide each one onto a cocktail stick. Top each cupcake with a tiny bow, being careful to keep the ribbon out of the icing. Keep for 2 days in an airtight container in a cool place. Remember to remove the cocktail sticks and bows before eating the cupcakes.

Sunflower Cupcakes

Makes 18

150 g/5 oz butter, softened
150 g/5 oz caster sugar
3 medium eggs, beaten
150 g/5 oz self-raising flour
$^1/_2$ tsp baking powder
zest and 2 tbsp juice of
1 small orange

To decorate

1 batch buttercream (see page 60)
yellow and orange food colourings

Preheat the oven to 180°C/350°F/Gas Mark 4 and line two bun trays with 18 paper fairy-cake cases.

Place the butter, sugar and beaten eggs in a bowl, then sift in the flour and baking powder. Finely grate the zest from the orange into the bowl and squeeze out 2 tablespoon juice.

Beat together for about 2 minutes, preferably with an electric hand–mixer, until pale and fluffy. Spoon the mixture into the paper cases and bake for about 15 minutes until firm and golden. Cool on a wire rack.

To decorate, colour three quarters of the buttercream bright yellow and the remainder orange. Place in two piping bags fitted with star nozzles. Pipe a border of straight lines round the outer edges to form petals. Pipe more petals to fill in the centres. Pipe a circle of orange dots in the centre of each to finish. Keep for 3 days in a cool place.

Red & White Cut-Out Heart Cakes

Makes 24

125 g/4 oz self-raising flour
125 g/4 oz caster sugar
125 g/4 oz soft margarine
2 medium eggs, beaten
1 tsp vanilla extract

To decorate

125 g/4 oz buttercream
(see page 60)
450 g/1 lb ready-to-roll sugarpaste
red paste food colouring

Preheat the oven to 180˚C/350˚F/Gas Mark 4. Line two 12-hole bun trays with paper or foil cases.

Sift the flour into a bowl and stir together with the caster sugar. Add the margarine and eggs and beat together with the vanilla extract for about 2 minutes. Spoon into the cases and bake for 15–20 minutes until golden and firm to the touch. Turn out on a wire rack. When cool, trim the tops flat.

To decorate, lightly coat the top of each cupcake with a little buttercream. Colour half the sugarpaste red. Dust a clean, flat surface with icing sugar. Roll out the sugarpaste and stamp out circles 6 cm/2^1/$_2$ inches wide. Place a small heart cutter centrally or trace round the pattern on page 250 and cut out heart shapes.

Carefully take a white outer circle and place it on the buttercream to cover the top of the cupcake. Take a palette knife and carefully position a red heart in the centre of the white icing. Press together and smooth over. Decorate all the cupcakes using alternate red and white backgrounds. Keep for 3 days in an airtight container in a cool place.

Bluebird Cupcakes

Makes 12–14

150 g/5 oz butter, softened
150 g/5 oz caster sugar
150 g/5 oz self-raising flour
3 medium eggs, beaten
1 tsp lemon juice
1 tbsp milk

To decorate

125 g/4 oz sugarpaste icing
blue paste food colouring
icing sugar, for dusting
1 batch cream cheese frosting
(see page 52)
white gel icing tube

Preheat the oven to 180°C/350°F/Gas Mark 4. Line a 12-hole tray with 12–14 deep paper cases, depending on the depth of the holes.

Place the butter and sugar in a bowl, then sift in the flour. Add the eggs to the bowl with the lemon juice and milk and beat until smooth. Spoon into the cases, filling them three-quarters full. Bake for about 18 minutes until firm to the touch in the centre. Turn out to cool on a wire rack.

To decorate the cupcakes, colour the sugarpaste blue. Dust a clean, flat surface with icing sugar. Roll out the sugarpaste thinly and mark out bird wings in sets of two and one body per bird. Trace round the patterns on page 252 and mark them onto the icing, then stamp out some daisy shapes. Leave all these to dry out for 30 minutes until firm enough to handle.

Swirl the frosting onto each cupcake. Press one bird's body and pair of wings, and some flowers, onto the frosting and pipe on decorations with the white gel icing tubes. Keep in an airtight container in a cool place for 3 days.

New Home Cupcakes

Makes 14

125 g/4 oz self-raising flour
125 g/4 oz caster sugar
125 g/4 oz soft margarine
2 medium eggs, beaten
1 tsp vanilla extract

To decorate

125 g/4 oz buttercream
(see page 60)
450 g/1 lb ready-to-roll sugarpaste
red, brown and yellow paste
food colourings
gel writing icing tubes

Preheat the oven to 180°C/350°F/Gas Mark 4. Line two 12-hole bun trays with 14 paper fairy-cake cases or silicone moulds.

Sift the flour into a bowl and stir together with the caster sugar. Add the margarine, eggs and vanilla extract and beat together for about 2 minutes until smooth. Spoon into the cases and bake for 15–20 minutes until golden and firm to the touch. Turn out on a wire rack. When cool, trim the tops flat if they have peaked slightly.

To decorate, lightly coat the top of each cupcake with a little buttercream. Dust a clean, flat surface with icing sugar. Colour half the sugarpaste a pale lemon yellow and roll it out thinly. Cut out circles 6 cm/21/2 inches wide and place these over the buttercream and press to smooth down. Colour half the remaining icing brown and the other half red. Roll out thinly on a dusted surface. Cut out small squares in the brown icing and then measure across and cut out a triangular roof shape in red icing. Press the shapes onto the cupcakes and pipe on doors, windows and roof tiles in white piping icing. Keep for 3 days in an airtight container.

Ruffled Cupcakes

Makes 12

125 g/4 oz self-raising flour
125 g/4 oz caster sugar
125 g/4 oz soft margarine
2 medium eggs, beaten
1 tsp lemon juice
1 tbsp milk

To decorate

125 g/4 oz buttercream
(see page 60)
450 g/1 lb ready-to-roll sugarpaste

Preheat the oven to 180°C/350°F/Gas Mark 4. Line a 12-hole bun tray with paper cases or silicone moulds.

Sift the flour into a bowl and stir together with the caster sugar. Add the margarine and eggs and beat together with the lemon juice and milk for about 2 minutes until smooth.

Spoon into the cases and bake for 15–20 minutes until golden and firm to the touch. Turn out on a wire rack. When cool, trim the tops flat if they have formed peaks. Spread buttercream over the flat surfaces.

To decorate, dust a clean flat, surface with icing sugar. Roll out the sugarpaste and stamp out a fluted circle 6 cm/2½ inches wide. Cut a 3 cm/1 inch wide circle out of the centre and discard. Take a cocktail stick and roll this back and forth in the sugarpaste circle until it begins to frill up. Take the frilled circle and place on the buttercream, fluting up the edges. Make another fluted circle and cut a break in the ring, then coil this round inside the first layer. Roll a pea-sized ball and place this in the centre. Serve dusted with icing sugar. Keep for 3 days in a cool place in an airtight container.

Shaggy Coconut Cupcakes

Makes 12

¹/₂ tsp baking powder
200 g/7 oz self-raising flour
175 g/6 oz caster sugar
2 tbsp desiccated coconut
175 g/6 oz soft margarine
3 medium eggs, beaten
2 tbsp milk

To decorate

1 batch buttercream
(see page page 60)
1 tbsp coconut liqueur (optional)
175 g/6 oz large shredded
coconut strands

Preheat the oven to 180°C/350°F/Gas Mark 4. Line a 12-hole, deep tray with paper cases.

Sift the baking powder and flour into a large bowl. Add all the remaining ingredients and beat for about 2 minutes until smooth and creamy. Divide evenly between the paper cases.

Bake for 18–20 minutes until risen, golden and firm to the touch. Leave in the tray for 2 minutes, then turn out to cool on a wire rack.

To decorate the cupcakes, if you are using the coconut liqueur, beat this into the buttercream, then swirl over each cupcake. To decorate, press large strands of shredded coconut into the buttercream. Keep for 3 days in an airtight container in a cool place.

Crystallised Violet Cupcakes

Makes 12

150 g/5 oz butter, softened
150 g/5 oz caster sugar
3 medium eggs, beaten
150 g/5 oz self-raising flour
½ tsp baking powder
1 lemon

To decorate

12 fresh violets
1 egg white
caster sugar
125 g/4 oz fondant icing sugar
pale violet food colouring

Preheat the oven to 180°C/350°F/Gas Mark 4 and line a 12-hole tray with deep paper cases.

Place the butter, sugar and eggs in a bowl. Sift in the flour and baking powder. Finely grate in the zest from the lemon.

Beat together for about 2 minutes with an electric hand-mixer until pale and fluffy. Spoon into the paper cases and bake for 20–25 minutes until firm and golden. Cool on a wire rack.

To decorate the cupcakes, spread the violets on some nonstick baking parchment. Beat the egg white until frothy, then brush thinly over the violets. Dust with caster sugar and leave to dry out for 2 hours. Beat the icing sugar with the colouring and enough water to give a thin coating consistency. Drizzle over the top of each cupcake quickly and top with a violet. Leave to set for 30 minutes. Store in an airtight container in a cool place. Keep for 2 days.

Cupcakes for
Kids' Parties

No children's party is complete without a mountain of brightly coloured cupcakes. Pirate Cupcakes are ideal for any adventurous youngster (or big kid!), while the Butterfly Wings and Flowers Cupcakes are perfect for bringing out kids' more creative side. Alternatively, let your imagination run wild with an explosion of decoration with some Glittery Outer Space Cupcakes!

Butterfly Wings & Flowers Cupcakes

Makes 12–14

150 g/5 oz butter, softened
150 g/5 oz caster sugar
175 g/5 oz self-raising flour
3 medium eggs, beaten
1 tsp lemon juice
2 tbsp milk

To decorate

350 g/12 oz ready-to-roll
sugarpaste
paste food colourings
icing sugar, for dusting
1 batch cream cheese frosting
(see page 52)
gel icing tubes

Preheat the oven to 180°C/350°F/Gas Mark 4. Line one or two 12-hole trays with 12–14 deep paper cases, depending on the depth of the holes.

Place the butter and sugar in a bowl, then sift in the flour. Add the beaten eggs to the bowl with the lemon juice and milk and beat until smooth. Spoon into the cases, filling them three-quarters full.

Bake for about 18 minutes until firm to the touch in the centre. Turn out to cool on a wire rack.

To decorate, colour the sugarpaste in batches of lilac, blue, pink and yellow. Dust a clean, flat surface with icing sugar. Roll out the sugarpaste thinly and mark out daisy shapes and butterfly wings following the pattern on page 252. Leave these to dry for 30 minutes until firm enough to handle.

Place the frosting in a piping bag fitted with a star nozzle and pipe swirls onto each cupcake. Press the wings and flowers onto the frosting and pipe on decorations with small gel icing tubes. Keep in an airtight container in a cool place for 3 days.

Pink Butterfly Cakes

Makes 12

150 g/5 oz butter,
softened at room temperature
150 g/5 oz caster sugar
3 medium eggs, beaten
1 tsp vanilla extract
150 g/5 oz self-raising flour
$^{1}/_{2}$ tsp baking powder

To decorate

pink and brown paste
food colourings
225 g/8 oz ready-to-roll
sugarpaste icing
1 batch cream cheese frosting
(see page 52)
tubes of gel writing icing

Preheat the oven to 180°C/350°F/Gas Mark 4 and line a 12-hole tray with deep paper cases.

Place the butter, sugar, eggs and vanilla extract in a bowl and then sift in the flour and baking powder. Beat together for about 2 minutes with an electric hand-mixer until pale and fluffy. Spoon into the paper cases and bake for 20–25 minutes until firm and golden. Cool on a wire rack.

To decorate, colour 200 g/7 oz of the sugarpaste pale pink and colour the remainder brown. Roll out the sugarpaste thinly and, using a cutter or the template on page 251, cut out four petal shapes for the wings for each cupcake and set them on nonstick baking parchment or clingfilm. Cut out 48 shapes altogether and leave to dry flat until firm (about 2 hours). Colour the cream cheese frosting bright pink and place in a piping bag fitted with a star nozzle.

Swirl pink icing on top of each cupcake, then press four wings on top of each. Mould the brown icing into body shapes and place on each cupcake. Pipe dots on the wings with tubes of gel writing icing. Keep for 2 days in an airtight container in a cool place.

Pink Party Piggies

Makes 12

125 g/4 oz caster sugar
125 g/4 oz soft tub margarine
2 medium eggs
1 tbsp milk
125 g/ 4 oz self-raising flour
$1/2$ tsp baking powder

To decorate

1 batch buttercream
(see page 60)
pink liquid food colouring
pink marshmallows
edible gold or silver balls

Preheat the oven to 190°C/375°F/Gas Mark 5. Line a bun tray with 12 small paper cases.

Place all the cupcake ingredients in a large bowl and beat with an electric mixer for about 2 minutes until smooth. Half-fill the paper cases with the mixture.

Bake for about 15 minutes until firm, risen and golden. Set on a wire rack to cool.

To decorate, mix the buttercream with the pink food colouring until it is pale pink. Spread smoothly over the top of each cupcake with a small palette knife. Cut a slice from a pink marshmallow with wetted scissors, then cut this in half to form the ears and press into the buttercream. Place a large, halved marshmallow in the centre to form the snout. Add edible gold or silver balls to form eyes. Keep for 2–3 days sealed in an airtight container.

Mini Cupcakes

Makes 24

100 g/3^1/$_2$ oz golden caster sugar
100 g/31/2 oz butter, softened
finely grated zest of ^{1}/$_2$ lemon and 1 tsp juice
2 medium eggs, beaten
100 g/3^1/$_2$ oz self-raising flour

To decorate

50 g/2 oz unsalted butter, softened
1 tsp vanilla extract
125 g/4 oz icing sugar, sifted
1 tbsp milk
paste food colouring
sugar sprinkles

Preheat the oven to 190°C/375°F/Gas Mark 5. Line a 24-hole mini tray with mini paper cases.

Put the sugar, butter and lemon zest in a large bowl and beat until light and fluffy. Beat in the egg a little at a time, adding a teaspoon of flour with each addition. Fold in the rest of the flour and the lemon juice and mix until smooth.

Spoon into the mini paper cases and bake for about 12 minutes until golden and risen. Transfer to a wire rack to cool.

To make the icing, beat the butter and vanilla extract together until light and fluffy, then gradually beat in the icing sugar and milk until a soft, easy-to-spread consistency has formed. Colour the icing in batches with paste food colourings, then spread over the cold cupcakes with a flat-bladed knife. Decorate with sugar sprinkles. Keep in an airtight container for 2 days.

Teddy Bear Cupcakes

Makes 14–16

125 g/4 oz self-raising flour
125 g/4 oz caster sugar
125 g/4 oz soft margarine
2 medium eggs, beaten
1 tsp vanilla extract

To decorate

225 g/8 oz ready-to-roll sugarpaste
brown paste food colouring
325 g/11$^{1}/_{2}$ oz fondant
icing sugar, plus extra
for dusting
6 tbsp royal icing sugar

Preheat the oven to 180°C/350°F/Gas Mark 4. Line two 12-hole bun trays with 14–16 paper fairy-cake cases or silicone moulds, depending on the depth of the holes. Sift the flour into a bowl and stir together with the caster sugar. Add the margarine, eggs and vanilla extract and beat together for about 2 minutes until smooth. Spoon into the cases and bake for 15–20 minutes until golden and firm to the touch. Turn out on a wire rack. When cool, trim the tops flat if they have peaked slightly.

Colour the sugarpaste brown. Dust a board with icing sugar. Roll the coloured sugarpaste thinly and stamp out bear shapes with a cutter or trace round the pattern on page 252 and mark onto the sugarpaste with a sharp knife. Leave to dry for 30 minutes.

Mix the fondant icing sugar with enough cold water to form a stiff, shiny icing of coating consistency and colour this light brown. Flood the icing on top of each cupcake and, while still wet, place a bear shape onto this. Mix the royal icing sugar with a little water to make a stiff paste and then pipe on eyes, a nose and buttons. Leave to set for 30 minutes. Keep for 1 day in an airtight container.

Kitty Faces Cupcakes

Makes 14–16

125 g/4 oz self-raising flour
125 g/4 oz caster sugar
125 g/4 oz soft margarine
2 medium eggs, beaten
1 tsp vanilla extract

To decorate

1 batch buttercream
(see page 60)
pink paste food colouring
50 g/2 oz desiccated coconut
Liquorice Allsorts sweets
red gel writing icing tube

Preheat the oven to 180°C/350°F/Gas Mark 4. Line two 12-hole bun trays with 12–14 paper fairy-cake cases or silicone moulds, depending on the depth of the holes.

Sift the flour into a bowl and stir together with the caster sugar. Add the margarine, eggs and vanilla extract and beat together for about 2 minutes until smooth.

Spoon into the cases and bake for 15–20 minutes until golden and firm to the touch. Turn out on a wire rack. When cool, trim the tops flat if they have peaked slightly.

Colour the buttercream pink and spread over the top of each cake. Pour the coconut onto a shallow dish. Press the top of each iced cupcake into the coconut. Cut the sweets to form pink ears, eyes, a jelly nose and whiskers and pipe on a red mouth in red gel icing. Keep in an airtight container in a cool place for 2 days.

Pirate Cupcakes

Makes 14–16

125 g/4 oz self-raising flour
125 g/4 oz caster sugar
125 g/4 oz soft margarine
2 medium eggs, beaten
1 tsp vanilla extract

To decorate

125 g/4 oz buttercream
(see page 60)
450 g/1 lb ready-to-roll sugarpaste
pink, yellow, blue and black paste
food colouring
small sweets and edible
coloured balls
small tube red gel icing

Preheat the oven to 180°C/350°F/Gas Mark 4. Line two 12-hole bun trays with 14–16 paper fairy-cake cases or silicone moulds, depending on the depth of the holes. Sift the flour into a bowl and stir together with the caster sugar. Add the margarine, eggs and vanilla extract and beat together for 2 minutes. Divide the mixture between the cases and bake for 15–20 minutes until golden and firm to the touch. Turn out on a wire rack. When cool, trim the tops.

To decorate, lightly coat the top of each cupcake with buttercream. Colour the sugarpaste pale pink and roll out thinly on a surface dusted with icing sugar. Stamp out circles 6 cm/2^1/$_2$ inches wide and place these on the buttercream on top of each cupcake. Colour some scraps of sugarpaste blue, some yellow and a small amount black. Make triangular shapes from the blue and yellow icing and place these onto the pink icing at an angle to form hats. Stick coloured edible balls into the icing to decorate the hats. Make thin sausages from the black icing and press these across the cupcakes, then make tiny eye patches from black icing. Stick on a tiny sweet for each eye and pipe on red mouths with the gel icing. Keep for 2 days in an airtight container.

Football Cupcakes

Makes 12–14

125 g/4 oz self-raising flour
125 g/4 oz caster sugar
125 g/4 oz soft margarine
2 medium eggs, beaten
1 tsp vanilla extract

To decorate

125 g/4 oz buttercream
(see page 60)
600 g/1 lb 5 oz ready-to-roll
sugarpaste
black paste food colouring

Preheat the oven to 180°C/350°F/Gas Mark 4. Line two 12-hole bun trays with 12–14 paper fairy-cake cases or silicone moulds, depending on the depth of the holes. Sift the flour into a bowl and stir together with the caster sugar. Add the margarine, eggs and vanilla extract and beat together for about 2 minutes until smooth. Spoon into the cases and bake for 15–20 minutes until golden and firm to the touch. Turn out on a wire rack. When cool, trim the tops flat if they have peaked slightly.

To decorate, lightly coat the top of each cupcake with a little buttercream. Roll out the white sugarpaste on a surface dusted with icing sugar and cut out circles 6 cm/2½ inches wide and place these on the buttercream to cover the top of each cupcake. Colour 75 g/3 oz of the scraps black.

Using a small icing nozzle as a round guide, stamp out small white and black discs. Cut six straight edges away from the circles to form hexagons. Dampen the back of each hexagon with a little water, then stick the black discs between white ones, carefully matching up all the edges so they fit together. Keep for 3 days in an airtight container.

Jellybean Cupcakes

Makes 12–14

125 g/4 oz self-raising flour
125 g/4 oz caster sugar
125 g/4 oz soft margarine
2 medium eggs, beaten
1 tsp vanilla extract

To decorate

1 batch buttercream
(see page 60)
colourful jellybeans or
candied jelly shapes

Preheat the oven to 180°C/350°F/Gas Mark 4. Line two 12-hole bun trays with 12–14 paper fairy-cake cases or silicone moulds, depending on the depth of the holes.

Sift the flour into a bowl and stir together with the caster sugar. Add the margarine, eggs and vanilla extract and beat together for about 2 minutes until smooth.

Spoon into the cases and bake for 15–20 minutes until golden and firm to the touch. Turn out to cool on a wire rack.

When completely cold, swirl buttercream icing all over the tops of the cupcakes and decorate by pressing on coloured jellybeans. Keep for 3 days in a cool place in an airtight container.

Fast Cars Cupcakes

Makes 12–14

125 g/4 oz self-raising flour
1 tbsp cocoa powder
125 g/4 oz caster sugar
125 g/4 oz soft margarine
2 medium eggs, beaten
1 tsp vanilla extract

To decorate

225 g/8 oz ready-to-roll sugarpaste
icing sugar, for dusting
red and blue paste food colourings
350 g/12 oz fondant icing
sugar, sifted
6 tbsp royal icing sugar

Preheat the oven to 180°C/350°F/Gas Mark 4. Line two 12-hole bun trays with 12–14 paper fairy-cake cases or silicone moulds, depending on the depth of the holes. Sift the flour and cocoa powder into a bowl and stir together with the caster sugar. Add the margarine, eggs and vanilla extract and beat together for about 2 minutes until smooth. Spoon into the cases and bake for 15–20 minutes until golden and firm to the touch. Turn out on a wire rack. When cool, trim the tops flat.

To decorate, colour half the sugarpaste blue and half red. Dust a clean surface lightly with icing sugar. Roll each colour out thinly and cut out little car shapes, tracing round the pattern on page 251. Leave these for 2 hours to dry and harden.

Blend the fondant icing sugar with enough water to make an icing to a coating consistency. Spread over the top of each cupcake and, while still wet, place a car shape in the centre of each one. Mix the royal icing sugar with enough water to make piping icing. Place in a small paper icing bag with the end snipped away. Pipe on wheels and windows and leave to dry for 30 minutes. Keep for 3 days in an airtight container.

Pink Flower Cupcakes

Makes 12

150 g/5 oz butter, softened
150 g/5 oz caster sugar
3 medium eggs, beaten
1 tsp vanilla extract
150 g /5 oz self-raising flour
$^1/_2$ tsp baking powder

To decorate

pink paste food colouring
650 g/1 lb 7 oz ready-to-roll
sugarpaste
$^1/_2$ batch cream cheese frosting
(see page 52)

Preheat the oven to 180°C/350°F/Gas Mark 4 and line a 12-hole tray with deep paper cases. Place the butter, sugar, eggs and vanilla extract in a bowl, then sift in the flour and baking powder. Beat together for about 2 minutes with an electric hand-mixer until pale and fluffy. Spoon into the paper cases and bake for 20–25 minutes until firm and golden. Cool on a wire rack.

To decorate the cupcakes, first line a 12-hole egg box with foil. Colour 175 g/6 oz of the sugarpaste pink. Roll it out thinly and cut out 12 flower shapes following the pattern on page 251. Use a cocktail stick to mark ridges on the petals and mould the icing in your hand to form flower shapes, then leave in the foil-lined egg boxes for 2 hours.

When the flowers are nearly hardened, roll out the remaining white sugarpaste thinly on a surface dusted with icing sugar and cut out circles 6 cm/2$^1/_2$ inches wide. Spread half the cream cheese frosting thinly over each cake and top with a sugarpaste disc. Top each cupcake with a flower, and pipe frosting into the centre of each. Keep in a sealed container in a cool place for up to 2 days.

Boys' ❦ Girls' Names

Makes 16–18

175 g/6 oz self-raising flour
175 g/6 oz caster sugar
175 g/6 oz soft margarine
3 medium eggs, beaten
1 tsp vanilla extract

To decorate

1 batch buttercream
(see page 60)
paste food colourings
sprinkles and decorations
gel writing icing tubes

Preheat the oven to 180°C/350°F/Gas Mark 4. Line two 12-hole bun trays with 16–18 paper fairy-cake cases or silicone moulds, depending on the depth of the holes.

Sift the flour into a bowl and stir together with the caster sugar. Add the margarine, eggs and vanilla extract and beat together for about 2 minutes until smooth.

Spoon into the cases and bake for 15–20 minutes until golden and firm to the touch. Turn out on a wire rack. When cool, trim the tops flat if they have peaked slightly.

Divide the buttercream into batches and colour them pink, green and yellow. Spread the icing over the cakes. Coat the edges of each cake with brightly coloured sprinkles, then add a name in the centre of each one with the writing icing. Keep in an airtight container in a cool place for 2 days.

Pink Candle Cupcakes

Makes 12

75 g/3 oz fresh raspberries
150 g/5 oz butter, softened
150 g/5 oz caster sugar
175 g/6 oz self-raising flour
3 medium eggs
1 tsp vanilla extract

To decorate

1 batch cream cheese frosting
(see page 52)
pink liquid food colouring
small pink candles

Preheat the oven to 180°C/350°F/Gas Mark 4. Line a 12-hole tray with deep paper cases.

Press the raspberries through the sieve to make a purée. Cream the butter and sugar together in a bowl, then sift in the flour. In another bowl, beat the eggs with the vanilla extract, then add to the butter and sugar mixture. Beat until smooth, then fold in the purée. Spoon into the cases, filling them three-quarters full.

Bake for about 18 minutes until firm to the touch in the centre. Turn out to cool on a wire rack.

Colour the frosting pink with a few dots of food colouring. Place in a piping bag fitted with a star nozzle and pipe large swirls on top of each cupcake. Top each cupcake with a tiny candle. Keep for 3 days in an airtight container in a cool place.

Raspberry Butterfly Cupcakes

Makes 12–14

125 g/4 oz caster sugar
125 g/4 oz soft tub margarine
2 medium eggs
125 g/4 oz self-raising flour
1/2 tsp baking powder
1/2 tsp vanilla extract

To decorate

4 tbsp seedless raspberry jam
12–14 fresh raspberries
icing sugar, to dust

Preheat the oven to 190°C/375°F/Gas Mark 5. Line one or two bun trays with 12–14 paper cases, depending on the depth of the holes.

Place all the cupcake ingredients in a large bowl and beat with an electric mixer for about 2 minutes until smooth. Fill the paper cases halfway up with the mixture.

Bake for about 15 minutes until firm, risen and golden. Remove to a wire rack to cool. When cold, cut a small circle out of the top of each cupcake and then cut the circle in half to form wings.

Fill each cupcake with a teaspoon of raspberry jam. Replace the wings at an angle and top each with a fresh raspberry. Dust lightly with icing sugar and serve immediately.

Polka Dot Cupcakes

Makes 12

150 g/5 oz butter, softened
150 g/5 oz caster sugar
175 g/6 oz self-raising flour
3 medium eggs
1 tsp vanilla extract
2 tbsp milk

To decorate

1 batch cream cheese frosting
(see page 52)
125 g/4 oz ready-to-roll
sugarpaste
paste food colourings

Preheat the oven to 180°C/350°F/Gas Mark 4. Line a 12-hole tray with paper cases.

Place the butter and sugar in a bowl, then sift in the flour. In another bowl, beat the eggs with the vanilla extract and milk, then add to the flour mixture and beat until smooth. Spoon into the cases, filling them three-quarters full.

Bake for about 18 minutes until firm to the touch in the centre. Turn out to cool on a wire rack.

To decorate the cupcakes, swirl the top of each cupcake with a little cream cheese frosting using a small palette knife. Divide the sugarpaste into batches and colour each one separately with paste food colouring. Dust a clean, flat surface with icing sugar. Roll out the coloured icing and stamp out small coloured circles with the flat end of an icing nozzle. Press the dots onto the frosting. Keep for 3 days in a cool place in an airtight container.

Starry Cupcakes

Makes 12

125 g/4 oz butter, softened
125 g/4 oz caster sugar
125 g/4 oz self-raising flour
2 medium eggs
1 tsp vanilla extract

To decorate

icing sugar, for dusting
225 g/8 oz ready-to-roll
sugarpaste
dust or paste food colourings
1 batch cream cheese frosting
(see page 52)
edible silver balls (optional)
small candles

Preheat the oven to 180°C/350°F/Gas Mark 4. Line a 12-hole tray with deep paper cases.

Place the butter and sugar in a bowl, then sift in the flour. In another bowl, beat the eggs with the vanilla extract, then add to the flour mixture. Beat until smooth, then spoon into the cases, filling them three-quarters full.

Bake for about 18 minutes until firm to the touch in the centre. Turn out to cool on a wire rack.

To decorate the cupcakes, dust a clean, flat surface with icing sugar. Colour the sugarpaste in batches of bright colours, such as blue, yellow and orange. Roll each out thinly and cut out stars with a cutter or follow the pattern on page 253. Leave to dry out for 2 hours until firm. Place the frosting in a piping bag fitted with a star nozzle and pipe large swirls on top of each cupcake. Decorate each cupcake with stars, edible silver balls, if using, and small candles. Keep for 2 days in an airtight container in a cool place.

Hearts ❧ Flowers Cupcakes

Makes 12

150 g/5 oz butter, softened
150 g/5 oz caster sugar
175 g/6 oz self-raising flour
3 medium eggs, beaten
1 tsp lemon juice
1 tbsp milk

To decorate

350 g/12 oz sugarpaste icing
paste food colourings
icing sugar, for dusting
1 batch cream cheese frosting
(see page 52)

Preheat the oven to 180°C/350°F/Gas Mark 4. Line a 12-hole tray with deep paper cases.

Place the butter and sugar in a bowl, then sift in the flour. Add the beaten eggs to the bowl with the lemon juice and milk and beat until smooth. Spoon into the cases, filling them three-quarters full.

Bake for about 18 minutes until firm to the touch in the centre. Turn out to cool on a wire rack.

To decorate, colour the sugarpaste in batches in any colours you like. Dust a clean, flat surface with icing sugar. Roll out the sugarpaste thinly and stamp out daisies using a flower stamp (based on the template on page 251), then roll out some more sugarpaste thinly and cut out small heart shapes using the template on see page 250. Leave these to dry out for 30 minutes until firm enough to handle.

Place the frosting in a piping bag fitted with a star nozzle. Pipe swirls onto each cupcake. Press the flowers and hearts onto the frosting. Keep in an airtight container in a cool place for 3 days.

Glittery Outer Space Cupcakes

Makes 18–20

125 g/4 oz soft margarine
125 g/4 oz caster sugar
125 g/4 oz self-raising flour
2 medium eggs
1 tsp vanilla extract
1 tbsp milk

To decorate

125 g/4 oz ready-to-roll sugarpaste
edible coloured or glitter dust
1 batch cream cheese frosting
(see page 52)
edible metallic coloured balls

Preheat the oven to 180°C/350°F/Gas Mark 4. Line a mini tray with 18–20 mini paper cases or silicone moulds, depending on the depth of the holes.

Place the margarine and sugar in a bowl, then sift in the flour. In another bowl, beat the eggs with the vanilla extract and milk, then add to the flour mixture. Beat until smooth, then spoon into the cases, filling them halfway up.

Bake for about 12–14 minutes until firm to the touch in the centre. Turn out to cool on a wire rack.

Place a large piece of nonstick baking parchment on a flat surface. Roll the sugarpaste into pea-sized balls on the paper. Coat the balls with edible coloured or glitter dust. Leave to dry out for 2 hours until firm. Place the frosting in a piping bag fitted with a star nozzle and pipe swirls on top of each cupcake. Top each cupcake with the coloured sugarpaste balls and edible metallic balls. Keep for 2 days in an airtight container in a cool place.

Seasonal
Celebration
Cupcakes

Cupcakes can simply and effortlessly add an extra magical touch to any special or seasonal occasion. Gingerbread Cupcakes are perfect for warming up a chilly winter's day, while Sparkly Snowflake Cupcakes make a great addition to any Christmas party. Let your green-fingered side show with Harvest Festival Cupcakes, or treat your loved one with the Valentine Heart Cupcakes.

Mini Valentine Heart Cupcakes

Makes 24

125 g/4 oz soft margarine
125 g/4 oz caster sugar
2 medium eggs, beaten
1 tsp vanilla extract
1 tbsp milk
125 g/4 oz self-raising flour

To decorate

pink and red paste food colourings
225 g/8 oz ready-to-roll sugarpaste
50 g/2 oz ready-made royal icing
1 batch cream cheese frosting
(see page 52)

Preheat the oven to 180°C/350°F/Gas Mark 4 and line a 24-hole mini tray with mini paper cases.

Place the margarine, sugar, eggs, vanilla extract and milk in a bowl, then sift in the flour. Beat together for about 2 minutes with an electric hand-mixer until pale and fluffy. Spoon into the paper cases and bake for 14–18 minutes until firm and golden. Cool on a wire rack.

To decorate, dust a clean, flat surface with icing sugar. Colour one third of the sugarpaste pink and one third red. Leave the rest white. Roll out the sugarpaste thinly and, using a cutter or the small heart template on page 250, cut out pink, red and white heart shapes. Press onto a cocktail stick and then secure with a little royal icing. Leave to dry flat and harden for 2 hours on greaseproof paper. Colour the cream cheese frosting pale pink and place in a piping bag fitted with a star nozzle.

Pipe a swirl on top of each cupcake and decorate each one with a heart. Keep in a cool place for up to 2 days. Remember to remove the cocktail sticks before eating the cupcakes.

Valentine Heart Cupcakes

Makes 12

150 g/5 oz butter, softened
150 g/5 oz caster sugar
3 medium eggs, beaten
1 tsp vanilla extract
2 tbsp milk
225 g/8 oz ready-to-roll sugarpaste
icing sugar, for dusting
1 batch cream cheese frosting
(see page 52)

Preheat the oven to 180°C/350°F/Gas Mark 4 and line a 12-hole tray with deep paper cases.

Place the butter, sugar, eggs, vanilla extract and milk in a bowl, then sift in the flour and baking powder. Beat together for about 2 minutes with an electric hand-mixer until pale and fluffy. Spoon into the paper cases and bake for 20–25 minutes until firm and golden. Cool on a wire rack.

To decorate, colour one third of the sugarpaste pink and one third red, leaving the rest white. Dust a clean, flat surface with icing sugar. Roll out the sugarpaste thinly and, using a cutter or the template on page 250, cut out pink, red and white heart shapes, then leave to dry flat and harden for 2 hours. Colour the cream cheese frosting pale pink and place in a piping bag fitted with a star nozzle.

Pipe a swirl on top of each cupcake and decorate with the hearts. Keep in a cool place for up to 2 days.

Mother's Day Rose Cupcakes

Makes 12

125 g/4 oz caster sugar
125 g/4 oz soft
tub margarine
2 medium eggs
125 g/4 oz self-raising flour
1 tsp baking powder
1 tsp rosewater

To decorate

50 g/2 oz ready-to-roll
sugarpaste
pink paste food colouring
350 g/12 oz fondant
icing sugar

Preheat the oven to 190°C/375°F/Gas Mark 5. Line a 12-hole bun tray with paper cases.

Place all the cupcake ingredients in a large bowl and beat with an electric mixer for about 2 minutes until smooth. Fill the paper cases halfway up with the mixture. Bake for about 15 minutes until firm, risen and golden. Remove to a wire rack to cool.

To decorate the cupcakes, first line an egg box with foil and set aside. Colour the sugarpaste with pink paste food colouring. Make a small cone shape, then roll a pea-sized piece of sugarpaste into a ball. Flatten out the ball into a petal shape and wrap this round the cone shape. Continue adding more petals to make a rose, then trim the thick base, place in the egg box and leave to dry out for 2 hours.

Blend the fondant icing sugar with a little water to make a thick icing of spreading consistency, then colour this pale pink. Smooth over the top of each cupcake and decorate with the roses immediately. Leave to set for 1 hour. Keep for 1 day in an airtight container.

Spring Daffodil Cupcakes

Makes 14

125 g/4 oz self-raising flour
125 g/4 oz caster sugar
125 g/4 oz soft margarine
2 medium eggs, beaten
1 tsp vanilla extract

To decorate

125 g/4 oz buttercream
(see page 60)
450 g/1 lb ready-to-roll sugarpaste
green, yellow and orange paste
food colourings

Preheat the oven to 180°C/350°F/Gas Mark 4. Line two 12-hole bun trays with 14 paper fairy-cake cases or silicone moulds. Sift the flour into a bowl and stir together with the caster sugar. Add the margarine, eggs and vanilla extract and beat together for about 2 minutes until smooth. Spoon into the cases and bake for 15–20 minutes until golden and firm to the touch. Turn out on a wire rack. When cool, trim the tops flat if they have peaked slightly.

To decorate the cupcakes, lightly coat the top of each with a little buttercream. Dust a clean, flat surface with icing sugar. Colour half the sugarpaste light green and roll out thinly. Stamp out circles 6 cm/21/2 inches wide and place these on the buttercream to cover the top of each cupcake.

Colour three quarters of the remaining icing yellow and a quarter orange. Roll out the yellow icing on some baking parchment and mark out thin petal shapes. Take 6 petals and pinch each one together. Place these onto the green icing in a circle, then mould a piece of orange icing into a pea-sized ball. Mould this into a cone shape and place in the centre of the flower. Keep for 3 days in an airtight container.

Easter Nest Cupcakes

Makes 12

125 g/4 oz soft margarine
125 g/4 oz golden caster sugar
150 g/5 oz self-raising flour
2 tbsp cocoa powder
2 medium eggs
1 tbsp golden syrup

To decorate

1 batch buttercream (see page 60)
50 g/2 oz shredded wheat cereal
125 g/4 oz milk chocolate, broken into pieces
25 g/1 oz unsalted butter
chocolate mini eggs

Preheat the oven to 180°C/350°F/Gas Mark 4. Line a 12-hole bun tray with paper cases.

Place the margarine and the sugar in a large bowl, then sift in the flour and cocoa powder. In another bowl, beat the eggs with the syrup, then add to the first bowl. Whisk together with an electric beater for 2 minutes, or by hand with a wooden spoon until smooth.

Divide the mixture between the cases, filling them three-quarters full. Bake for about 15 minutes until they are springy to the touch in the centre. Turn out to cool on a wire rack.

To decorate, swirl the buttercream over the top of each cupcake. Break up the shredded wheat finely. Melt the chocolate with the butter, then stir in the shredded wheat and let cool slightly. Line a plate with clingfilm. Mould the mixture into tiny nest shapes with your fingers, then place them on the lined plate. Freeze for a few minutes to harden. Set a nest on top of each cupcake and fill with mini eggs. Keep for 2 days in a cool place in an airtight container.

Christening Day Daisy Cupcakes

Makes 12

150 g/5 oz butter, softened
150 g/5 oz caster sugar
150 g/5 oz self-raising flour
3 medium eggs, beaten
1 tsp lemon juice
2 tbsp milk

To decorate

icing sugar, for dusting
125 g/4 oz sugarpaste
yellow gel icing tube
1 batch cream cheese frosting
(see page 52)
yellow paste food colouring

Preheat the oven to 180°C/350°F/Gas Mark 4. Line a 12-hole tray with deep paper cases.

Place the butter and sugar in a bowl, then sift in the flour. Add the beaten eggs to the bowl with the lemon juice and milk and beat until smooth. Spoon into the cases, filling them three-quarters full.

Bake for about 18 minutes until firm to the touch in the centre. Turn out to cool on a wire rack.

To decorate, dust a clean, flat surface with icing sugar. Roll out the sugarpaste thinly and stamp out daisy shapes. Leave these to dry out for 30 minutes until firm enough to handle. Pipe a small yellow gel dot into the centre of each one. Colour the frosting pale yellow, then spread onto the cakes using a palette knife. Press the daisies onto the frosting. Keep in an airtight container in a cool place for 3 days.

Silver Wedding Celebration Cakes

Makes 24

150 g/5 oz butter, softened
150 g/5 oz caster sugar
150 g/5 oz self-raising flour
25 g/1 oz ground almonds
3 medium eggs, beaten
1 tsp almond extract
2 tbsp milk

To decorate

350 g/12 oz sugarpaste
edible silver dusting powder
450 g/1 lb fondant icing sugar
24 small silver ribbon bows

Preheat the oven to 180°C/350°F/Gas Mark 4. Line two 12-hole bun trays with silver foil cases. Place the butter and sugar in a bowl, sift in the flour and stir in the almonds. Add the beaten eggs to the bowl along with the almond extract and milk, beat until smooth. Spoon into the cases, then bake for about 18 minutes until firm to the touch in the centre. Turn out onto a wire rack. Once cool, trim the tops if peaked.

To decorate, roll the sugarpaste into pea-sized balls and mould each one into a petal shape. Mould a cone shape and wrap a petal round this. Take another petal and wrap round the first, overlapping. Continue wrapping 4–5 petals round until a rose has formed; flute out the petals. Repeat until you have 24 roses. Leave them to dry out for 2–4 hours. When firm, brush edible silver dust lightly over each rose.

Mix the fondant icing sugar with water, according to the packet instructions, to a thick icing of a spreading consistency. Spread over the top of each cupcake. Work quickly, as this icing will set rapidly. Press a rose into the icing and place a thin silver bow on each cupcake. Leave to set for 30 minutes. Keep in a cool place for 2 days. Remove bows before eating.

Golden Wedding Celebration Cakes

Makes 24

125 g/4 oz self-raising flour
125 g/4 oz caster sugar
125 g/4 oz soft margarine
2 medium eggs, beaten
1 tsp lemon juice

To decorate

125 g/4 oz buttercream
(see page 60)
icing sugar, for dusting
700 g/1¹/₂ lb ready-to-roll
sugarpaste
yellow paste food colouring
thin gold ribbon

Preheat the oven to 180°C/350°F/Gas Mark 4. Line two 12-hole bun trays with small gold foil cases. Sift the flour into a bowl and stir together with the caster sugar. Add the margarine and eggs and beat together with the lemon juice for 2 minutes until smooth. Spoon into the cases and bake for 15–20 minutes until golden and firm to the touch. Turn out on a wire rack. When cool, trim the tops flat if they have peaked slightly.

To decorate, lightly coat the top of each cupcake with buttercream. Dust a clean, flat surface with icing sugar. Roll out two thirds of the sugarpaste and stamp out circles 6 cm/2¹/₂ inches wide and place these on the buttercream on top of each cupcake.

Colour one eighth of the sugarpaste yellow and mould this into thin sticks. Leave to dry for about 2 hours. Roll out the remaining white sugarpaste and mark out small squares 4 x 4 cm (1¹/₂ x 1¹/₂ inch). Wrap a square round a yellow stick to form a lily and press the ends together. Make up all the lilies and place on the cupcakes. Pull short, thin strips of gold paper ribbon along a scissor blade to curl, and place on the cakes. Keep for 3 days in an airtight container in a cool place. Remove the ribbons before eating.

Pink Baby Bow Cupcakes

Makes 12

125 g/4 oz self-raising flour
125 g/4 oz caster sugar
125 g/4 oz soft margarine
2 medium eggs, beaten
1 tsp vanilla extract
pink paste food colouring

To decorate

1 batch buttercream
(see page 60)
pink paste food colouring
225 g/8 oz ready-to-roll sugarpaste

Preheat the oven to 180°C/350°F/Gas Mark 4. Line a 12-hole tray with deep paper cases or silicone moulds. Sift the flour into a bowl and stir together with the caster sugar. Add the margarine, eggs and vanilla extract and beat together with a little pink paste food colouring to give a delicate pink. Beat for about 2 minutes until smooth. Spoon into the cases and bake for 20 minutes. Turn out on a wire rack. When cool, trim the tops flat if peaked.

To decorate, colour the buttercream pale pink, then colour the sugarpaste pink to match the buttercream. Dust a clean, flat surface with icing sugar. Roll out the sugarpaste thinly and cut out long, narrow strips 1¹/₂ cm/¹/₂ inch wide. Roll small squares of nonstick baking parchment into narrow tubes and fold the pink icing over these to form loops. Make 24 loops, two for each cupcake, and leave to dry for 2 hours. Cut strips to form the ribbon ends of each bow and set aside on nonstick baking parchment. To finish off the cupcakes, spread the top of each one with pink buttercream, carefully remove the loops from the paper and position the bows on the icing. Place the ribbon pieces onto the cupcakes to finish. Keep for 3 days in a cool place in an airtight container.

Father's Day Cupcakes

Makes 14

125 g/4 oz self-raising flour
125 g/4 oz caster sugar
125 g/4 oz soft margarine
2 medium eggs, beaten
1 tsp vanilla extract

To decorate

1 batch buttercream
(see page 60)
blue, yellow and orange paste
food colourings
225 g/8 oz ready-to-roll
sugarpaste
50 g/2 oz royal icing sugar
edible silver balls

Preheat the oven to 180°C/350°F/Gas Mark 4. Line two 12-hole bun trays with 14 paper fairy-cake cases or silicone moulds.

Sift the flour into a bowl and stir together with the caster sugar. Add the margarine, eggs and vanilla extract and beat together for about 2 minutes until smooth. Spoon into the cases and bake for 15–20 minutes until golden and firm to the touch. Turn out on a wire rack. When cool, trim the tops flat if they have peaked slightly.

To decorate, colour half the buttercream yellow and the other half orange and swirl over the top of each cupcake. Dust a clean, flat surface with icing sugar. Colour the sugarpaste light blue and roll out thinly. Stamp out large stars 4 cm/1^1/$_2$ inches wide using the template on page 253 and place these on the buttercream. Make up the royal icing mix and place in a paper piping bag with the end snipped away and pipe 'Dad' or names on the stars. Decorate with the edible silver balls. Keep for 3 days in an airtight container.

Chocolate ❧ Cranberry Cupcakes

Makes 12

125 g/4 oz soft margarine
125 g/4 oz golden
caster sugar
2 medium eggs
175 g/6 oz self-raising flour
25 g/1 oz cocoa powder
1 tsp baking powder
2 tbsp milk
125 g/4 oz milk chocolate chips
50 g/2 oz dried cranberries

To decorate

25 g/1 oz cocoa powder
40 g/1½ oz unsalted butter
125 g/4 oz golden icing sugar
25 g/1 oz dried cranberries

Preheat the oven to 180°C/350°F/Gas Mark 4. Line a 12-hole tray with deep paper cases.

Place the margarine, sugar and eggs in a bowl, then sift in the flour, cocoa powder and baking powder. Add the milk and beat until smooth, then fold in the chocolate chips and cranberries.

Spoon into the paper cases and bake for 15–20 minutes until firm in the centre. Remove to a wire rack to cool.

To decorate the cupcakes, blend the cocoa powder with 1 tablespoon hot water until smooth. Cool for 5 minutes. Beat the butter and icing sugar together and then beat in the cocoa mixture. Place in a piping bag with a plain nozzle and pipe swirls on top of each cupcake. Top with dried cranberries. Keep for 2–3 days in the refrigerator.

Halloween Cobweb Cupcakes

Makes 16–18

175 g/6 oz caster sugar
175 g/6 oz soft margarine
3 medium eggs, beaten
150 g/5 oz self-raising flour
1 tsp baking powder
25 g/1 oz cocoa powder

To decorate

225 g/8 oz icing sugar, sifted
2 tbsp warm water
orange and black paste
food colourings

Preheat the oven to 180°C/350°F/Gas Mark 4. Line two 12-hole bun trays with 16–18 paper or foil cases, depending on the depth of the holes. Place the sugar, margarine and eggs in a bowl, then sift in the flour, baking powder and cocoa powder. Beat for 2 minutes, or until smooth. Spoon the mixture into the paper cases and bake for 15–20 minutes until well risen and the tops spring back when lightly pressed. Transfer to a wire rack to cool, then trim the tops of the cupcakes flat if they are peaked.

To decorate the cupcakes, gradually mix the icing sugar with enough warm water to give a coating consistency. Colour a little of the icing black and place in a small paper icing bag. Colour the remaining icing bright orange.

Work on one cupcake at a time. Spread orange icing over the top of the cupcake. Snip a small hole from the base of the icing bag, then pipe a black spiral on top of the wet orange icing. Pull a wooden cocktail stick through the icing to give a cobweb effect. Repeat with all the cupcakes and leave to set for 1 hour. Keep for 2 days in an airtight container in a cool place.

Harvest Festival Cupcakes

Makes 12

175 g/6 oz self-raising
wholemeal flour
1 tsp baking powder
½ tsp ground cinnamon
pinch salt
150 ml/¼ pint sunflower oil
150 g/5 oz soft light
brown sugar
3 medium eggs, beaten
1 tsp vanilla extract
50 g/2 oz sultanas
225 g/8 oz carrots, peeled and
finely grated

To decorate

1 batch cream cheese frosting
(see page 52)
paste food colourings
225 g/8 oz ready-to-roll sugarpaste

Preheat the oven to 180°C/350°F/Gas Mark 4. Lightly oil a deep, 12-hole tray or line with deep paper cases.

Sift the flour, baking powder, cinnamon and salt into a bowl, along with any bran from the sieve. Add the oil, sugar, eggs, vanilla extract, sultanas and grated carrots.

Beat until smooth and then spoon into the tray. Bake for 20–25 minutes until risen and golden. Cool on a wire rack.

To decorate, colour the frosting pale green and smooth over the top of each cupcake. Colour the sugarpaste in small batches of orange, red, green and brown and mould into cabbages, carrots, potatoes and tomatoes. Press green sugarpaste through a garlic press to make green carrot leaves. Place the vegetables on top of each cupcake. Keep for 3 days in an airtight container in a cool place.

Scandinavian Apple Cupcakes

Makes 12–14

125 g/4 oz self-raising flour
1/2 tsp ground cinnamon
125 g/4 oz caster sugar
125 g/4 oz soft margarine
2 medium eggs, beaten
1 tsp vanilla extract

To decorate

125 g/4 oz buttercream
(see page 60)
600 g/1 lb 5 oz ready-to-roll
sugarpaste
red, green and brown paste
food colourings

Preheat the oven to 180°C/350°F/Gas Mark 4. Line two 12-hole bun trays with red paper or foil cases.

Sift the flour and cinnamon into a bowl and stir together with the caster sugar. Add the margarine and eggs and beat together with the vanilla extract for about 2 minutes until smooth.

Spoon into the cases and bake for 15–20 minutes until golden and firm to the touch. Turn out to cool on a wire rack. When cool, trim the tops flat if they have peaked slightly.

To decorate, lightly coat the top of each cupcake with a little buttercream. Dust a clean, flat surface with icing sugar. Colour one quarter of the sugarpaste red, one quarter green and a few scraps brown, leaving the rest white. Roll out the white sugarpaste and stamp out circles 6 cm/2 1/2 inches wide. Place on top of each cupcake and smooth level. Mould the green and red sugarpaste into round apple shapes and place on top of the white icing. Decorate with small green leaves and brown stalks. Keep for 3 days in an airtight container in a cool place.

Sparkly Snowflake Cupcakes

Makes 24

150 g/5 oz butter, softened
150 g/5 oz caster sugar
150 g/5 oz self-raising flour
25 g/1 oz ground almonds
3 medium eggs, beaten
1 tsp almond extract
1 tbsp milk

To decorate

icing sugar, for dusting
350 g/12 oz sugarpaste
450 g/1 lb royal icing sugar
edible silver balls

Preheat the oven to 180°C/350°F/Gas Mark 4. Line two 12-hole bun trays with silver foil cases. Place the butter and sugar in a bowl, then sift in the flour and stir in the almonds. Add the beaten eggs to the bowl with the almond extract and milk. Spoon into the cases, filling them three-quarters full.

Bake for about 18 minutes until firm to the touch in the centre. Turn out onto a wire rack. Once cool, trim the tops of the cupcakes if peaked.

To decorate the cupcakes, dust a clean, flat surface with icing sugar. Roll the sugarpaste thinly and trace round the snowflake pattern on page 252. Cut round the shapes and leave them to dry flat on a sheet of nonstick baking parchment for 2 hours.

Make up the royal icing sugar according to the packet instructions to a soft icing that will form peaks. Swirl the icing onto the cupcakes and place a snowflake shape centrally on each cupcake. Decorate with silver balls and leave for 30 minutes to set. Keep for 2 days in an airtight container.

Christmas Rose Cupcakes

Makes 18

150 g/5 oz butter, softened
150 g/5 oz caster sugar
150 g/5 oz self-raising flour
25 g/1 oz ground almonds
3 medium eggs, beaten
1 tsp almond extract
2 tbsp milk

To decorate

350 g/12 oz sugarpaste
450 g/1 lb fondant icing sugar
125 g/4 oz ready-made
royal icing
yellow paste food colouring

Preheat the oven to 180°C/350°F/Gas Mark 4. Line two 12-hole bun trays with 18 silver foil cases. Place the butter and sugar in a bowl, then sift in the flour and stir in the almonds. Add the beaten eggs to the bowl with the almond extract and milk and beat until smooth. Spoon into the cases, filling them three-quarters full.

Bake for about 18 minutes until firm to the touch in the centre. Turn out onto a wire rack. Once cool, trim the tops of the cupcakes if peaked.

To decorate the cupcakes, roll the sugarpaste into pea-sized balls and mould each one into a petal shape. Make 4–5 petals for each cupcake. Allow to dry for 2 hours until firm. Mix the fondant icing sugar with water, according to the packet instructions, to a thick icing of a spreading consistency. Spread over the top of each cupcake. Work quickly, as the icing will start to set rapidly. Press 4–5 petals into the icing on each cupcake. Colour the royal icing pale lemon and place in a small paper icing bag and snip off the end. Pipe dots in the centre of each flower and leave to set for 30 minutes. Keep in a cool place for 2 days.

Winter Wedding Cupcakes

Makes 12–14

125 g/4 oz butter
125 g/4 oz soft dark muscovado sugar
2 medium eggs, beaten
225 g/8 oz self-raising flour
1 tsp ground mixed spice
finely grated zest and 1 tbsp juice from 1 orange
1 tbsp black treacle
350 g/12 oz mixed dried fruit

To decorate

3 tbsp sieved apricot glaze (see page 64)
450 g/1 lb almond paste (see page 62)
icing sugar, for dusting
225 g/8 oz ready-to-roll sugarpaste
225 g/8 oz royal icing
fancy paper wrappers (optional)

Preheat the oven to 180˚C/350˚F/Gas Mark 4. Line one or two 12-hole trays with 12–14 deep paper cases. Beat the butter and sugar together until light and fluffy, then beat in the eggs a little at a time, adding 1 teaspoon flour with each addition. Sift in the remaining flour and the spice, add the orange zest and juice, the treacle and dried fruit to the bowl and fold together until the mixture is blended. Spoon into the trays and bake for 30 minutes. Leave to cool in the trays for 15 minutes, then turn out onto a wire rack. Store undecorated in an airtight container for up to 3 weeks, or freeze until needed.

To decorate the cupcakes, trim the top of each cake level, then brush with apricot glaze. Roll out the almond paste and cut out eight discs 6 cm/2¹/₂ inches wide. Place these over the glaze and press level. Leave to dry for 24 hours. Dust a clean, flat surface with icing sugar. Roll out the sugarpaste and stamp out holly leaf and ivy shapes, using the patterns on pages 250 and 251. Leave to dry for 2 hours. Swirl the royal icing over the top of each cupcake. Press in the holly and ivy shapes and leave to set for 2 hours. Once decorated, keep in an airtight container for 3 days.

Festive Candy Cane Cupcakes

Makes 14–18

150 g/5 oz butter, softened
150 g/5 oz caster sugar
150 g/5 oz self-raising flour
25 g/1 oz ground almonds
3 medium eggs, beaten
1 tsp vanilla extract
2 tbsp milk

To decorate

225 g/8 oz sugarpaste
red and green paste
food colourings
450 g/1 lb royal icing sugar

Preheat the oven to 180°C/350°F/Gas Mark 4. Line two 12-hole bun trays with 14–18 foil cases, depending on the depth of the holes. Place the butter and sugar in a bowl, sift in the flour and stir in the almonds. Add the eggs to the bowl along with the vanilla extract and milk. Spoon into the cases, filling them three-quarters full. Bake for about 18 minutes until firm to the touch in the centre. Turn out onto a wire rack. Once cool, trim the tops if peaked.

To decorate, colour one quarter of the sugarpaste red and one quarter green. Dust a clean, flat surface with icing sugar. Roll out the sugarpaste into long sticks with the palms of your hands. Roll a stick of red with a stick of white to form a twist. Cut into short lengths about 5 cm/2½ inches long and bend to form a cane shape. Leave to dry for 2 hours.

Make up the royal icing according to the packet instructions to a soft icing that will form peaks. Smooth the icing onto the cupcakes and place a cane centrally on each cupcake. Place the remaining icing in a small piping bag fitted with a star nozzle and pipe a star border round the outside of each cupcake. Keep for 2 days in an airtight container.

Sparkly Christmas Cupcakes

Makes 14–18

125 g/4 oz butter, softened
125 g/4 oz soft dark
muscovado sugar
2 medium eggs, beaten
225 g/8 oz self-raising flour
1 tsp ground mixed spice
finely grated zest and 1 tbsp juice
from 1 orange
1 tbsp black treacle
350 g/12 oz mixed dried fruit

To decorate

3 tbsp sieved apricot glaze
(see page 64)
225 g/8 oz almond paste
(see page 62)
1 batch royal icing
(see page 54)
edible silver balls

Preheat the oven to 180˚C/350˚F/Gas Mark 4. Line a 12-hole bun tray with 14–18 foil fairy-cake cases, depending on the size of the holes. Beat the butter and sugar together until light and fluffy, then beat in the eggs a little at a time, adding 1 teaspoon flour with each addition. Sift in the remaining flour and spice, add the orange zest and juice, treacle and dried fruit to the bowl and fold together until the mixture is blended. Spoon into the cases and bake for about 30 minutes. Leave to cool in the trays for 15 minutes, then turn out to cool on a wire rack. Store undecorated in an airtight container for up to 3 weeks, or freeze until needed.

To decorate, trim the top of each cake level, if they have peaked, then brush with apricot glaze. Roll out the almond paste and, using the circle on page 252 as a guide, cut out eight circles. Place a disc on top of each cake and press level. Leave to dry for 24 hours if possible.

Swirl the royal icing over the cakes, flicking into peaks with a palette knife. Use silver balls to decorate while the icing is still wet. Leave to dry for 1 hour. Keep for 4 days in an airtight container.

Honey Spice Cupcakes

ℰ

Makes 12–14

1 tsp instant coffee granules
6 tbsp hot water
175 g/6 oz plain flour
1 tsp baking powder
1/2 tsp bicarbonate of soda
1/2 tsp ground cinnamon
1/2 tsp ground ginger
pinch ground cloves
2 medium eggs
125 g/4 oz golden caster sugar
175 g/6 oz honey
5 tbsp vegetable oil
50 g/2 oz walnuts, finely chopped
125 g/4 oz golden icing sugar,
to decorate

Preheat the oven to 160°C/325°F/Gas Mark 3. Line one or two trays with 12–14 deep paper cases, depending on the depth of the holes. Dissolve the coffee in the water and leave aside to cool.

Sift the flour with the baking powder, bicarbonate of soda and spices. In another bowl, beat the eggs with the sugar and honey until smooth and light, then gradually beat in the oil until blended. Stir this into the flour mixture along with the coffee and walnuts. Beat until smooth.

Carefully spoon the mixture into the paper cases. Fill each halfway up. Take care not to overfill them, as the mixture will rise up. Bake for 25–30 minutes until they are risen, firm and golden. Leave in the trays for 5 minutes, then turn out onto a wire rack to cool.

To decorate, blend the icing sugar with 1 tablespoon warm water to make a thin glacé icing. Place in a paper icing bag and snip away the tip. Pipe large daisies round the sides of each cupcake and leave to set for 30 minutes. Keep in an airtight container for up to 5 days.

Chocolate Holly Leaf Cupcakes

Makes 12

125 g/4 oz caster sugar
125 g/4 oz soft tub margarine
2 medium eggs
125 g/4 oz self-raising flour
$^{1}/_{2}$ tsp baking powder
50 g/2 oz plain or milk
chocolate chips

To decorate

12 holly leaves, washed and dried
75 g/3 oz dark
chocolate, melted
50 g/2 oz unsalted
butter, softened
300 g/11 oz icing sugar, sifted
125 g/4 oz full-fat cream cheese
50 g/2 oz milk chocolate, melted
and cooled
1 tsp vanilla extract

Preheat the oven to 190°C/375°F/Gas Mark 5. Line a 12-hole tray with deep paper cases. Place all the cupcake ingredients except the chocolate chips in a large bowl and beat with an electric mixer for about 2 minutes. Fold in the chocolate chips, then fill the paper cases with the mixture. Bake for about 15 minutes. Remove to a wire rack to cool.

To decorate, paint the underside of each holly leaf with melted dark chocolate. Leave to dry for 1 hour, or in the refrigerator for 30 minutes. Beat the butter until soft, then gradually beat in the icing sugar until light. Add the cream cheese and whisk until fluffy. Divide the mixture in half and beat the cooled melted milk chocolate into one half and the vanilla extract into the other. Fit a piping bag with a wide star nozzle and spoon chocolate frosting on one side of the bag and the vanilla frosting on the other. Pipe swirls on top of the cupcakes.

Peel the leaves away from the set chocolate and decorate the top of each cupcake with a leaf. Keep for 3 days in an airtight container in a cool place.

Gingerbread Cupcakes

Makes 14–16

8 tbsp golden syrup
125 g/4 oz block margarine
225 g/8 oz plain flour
2 tsp ground ginger
75 g/3 oz sultanas
50 g/2 oz soft dark
brown sugar
175 ml/6 fl oz milk
1 tsp bicarbonate of soda
1 medium egg, beaten
125 g/4 oz golden icing sugar,
to decorate

Preheat the oven to 180°C/350°F/Gas Mark 4. Line one or two trays with 14–16 deep paper cases, depending on the size of the holes.

Place the syrup and margarine in a heavy-based pan and melt together gently. Sift the flour and ginger into a bowl, then stir in the sultanas and sugar.

Warm the milk and stir in the bicarbonate of soda. Pour the syrup mixture, the milk and the beaten egg into the dry ingredients and beat until smooth.

Spoon the mixture halfway up each case and bake for 25–30 minutes until risen and firm. Cool in the trays for 10 minutes, then turn out to cool on a wire rack.

To decorate the cupcakes, blend the icing sugar with 1 tablespoon warm water to make a thin glacé icing. Place in a paper icing bag and snip away the tip. Drizzle over the top of each cupcake in a lacy pattern. Keep in an airtight container for up to 5 days.

Hogmanay Party Cupcakes

Makes 14

125 g/4 oz self-raising flour
125 g/4 oz caster sugar
125 g/4 oz soft margarine
2 medium eggs, beaten
1 tsp vanilla extract

To decorate

125 g/4 oz buttercream
(see page 60)
450 g/1 lb ready-to-roll sugarpaste
yellow, green and lilac paste food
colourings

Preheat the oven to 180°C/350°F/Gas Mark 4. Line two 12-hole bun trays with 14 paper fairy-cake cases or silicone moulds. Sift the flour into a bowl and stir together with the caster sugar. Add the margarine and eggs. Beat with the vanilla extract for about 2 minutes until smooth. Spoon into the cases and bake for 15–20 minutes until golden and firm to the touch. Turn out onto a wire rack. When cool, trim the tops.

To decorate, lightly coat the top of each cake with a little buttercream. Dust a clean, flat surface with icing sugar. Colour half the sugarpaste a pale cream shade and roll out thinly. Stamp out circles 6 cm/2½ inches wide and place these on the buttercream to cover the top of each cake.

Colour the remaining icing green and lilac. Mould the green icing into stems. Mark the bulbous parts of the stems with 'spikes', and position on the cakes. Roll out the lilac sugarpaste into a long, thin strip about 2.5 cm/1 inch wide. Cut with a knife, or snip with scissors, three quarters of the way through the paste, then roll up to form a tassel for a thistle top and attach to the top of a stem. Repeat on all the cakes. Keep for 3 days in an airtight container.

Giftwrapped Presents Cupcakes

Makes 12–14

125 g/4 oz butter
125 g/4 oz soft dark
muscovado sugar
2 medium eggs, beaten
225 g/8 oz self-raising flour
1 tsp ground mixed spice
finely grated zest and 1 tbsp juice
from 1 orange
1 tbsp black treacle
350 g/12 oz mixed dried fruit

To decorate

3 tbsp sieved apricot glaze
(see page 64)
icing sugar, for dusting
600 g/1 lb 5 oz ready-to-roll
sugarpaste
red, blue, green and yellow paste
food colourings

Preheat the oven to 180°C/350°F/Gas Mark 4. Line one or two 12-hole trays with 12–14 deep paper cases, depending on the depth of the holes. Beat the butter and sugar together until light and fluffy, then beat in the eggs a little at a time, adding 1 teaspoon flour with each addition. Sift in the remaining flour and spice, add the orange zest and juice, treacle and dried fruit to the bowl and fold together until the mixture is blended. Spoon into the cases and bake for about 30 minutes until firm in the centre and a skewer comes out clean. Leave to cool in the trays for 15 minutes, then turn out to cool on a wire rack. Store undecorated in an airtight container for up to 4 weeks, or freeze.

To decorate, trim the top of each cupcake level, then brush with apricot glaze. Dust a clean, flat surface with icing sugar. Colour the sugarpaste in batches and roll out thinly. Cut out circles 6 cm/2^1/$_2$ inches wide. Place a disc on top of each cupcake and press level. Mould coloured scraps into long, thin sticks and roll these out thinly. Place a contrasting colour across each cupcake and arrange into bows and loops. Leave to dry for 24 hours. Keep for 4 days in an airtight container.

Rosemary ❧ Cranberry Cupcakes

Makes 12

125 g/4 oz self-raising flour
125 g/4 oz butter, softened
125 g/4 oz golden caster sugar
2 medium eggs, beaten
zest of $1/2$ orange,
finely grated

To decorate

1 egg white
12 small rosemary sprigs
125 g/4 oz fresh cranberries
caster sugar, for dusting
3 tbsp apricot glaze, sieved
(see page 64)
350 g/12 oz ready-to-roll
sugarpaste

Preheat the oven to 180°C/350°F/Gas Mark 4. Line a 12-hole bun tray with foil fairy-cake cases.

Sift the flour into a bowl and add the butter, sugar, eggs and orange zest. Beat for about 2 minutes until smooth, then spoon into the paper cases.

Bake in the centre of the oven for about 14 minutes until well risen and springy in the centre. Transfer to a wire rack to cool.

To decorate, place a sheet of nonstick baking parchment on a flat surface. Beat the egg white until frothy, then brush thinly over the rosemary and cranberries and place them on the nonstick baking parchment. Dust with caster sugar and leave to dry out for 2–4 hours until crisp.

Brush the top of each cake with a little apricot glaze. Roll out the sugarpaste on a clean, flat surface dusted with icing sugar and cut out 12 circles 6 cm/$2^1/2$ inches wide. Place a disc on top of each and press level. Decorate each one with sparkly rosemary sprigs and cranberries. Keep for 3 days in an airtight container in a cool place.

Christmas Tree Cupcakes

ℰ

Makes 14

125 g/4 oz self-raising flour
125 g/4 oz caster sugar
125 g/4 oz soft margarine
2 medium eggs, beaten
1 tsp vanilla extract

To decorate

125 g/4 oz buttercream
(see page 60)
600 g/1 lb 5 oz ready-to-roll
sugarpaste
green paste food colouring
edible silver balls

Preheat the oven to 180°C/350°F/Gas Mark 4. Line two 12-hole bun trays with 14 paper fairy-cake cases or silicone moulds. Sift the flour into a bowl and stir together with the caster sugar. Add the margarine, eggs and vanilla extract and beat together for about 2 minutes until smooth. Spoon into the cases and bake for 15–20 minutes until golden and firm to the touch. Turn out onto a wire rack. When cool, trim the tops flat if they have peaked slightly.

To decorate, lightly coat the top of each cake with a little buttercream. Colour one quarter of the sugarpaste green and set aside. Dust a clean, flat surface with icing sugar. Roll the white sugarpaste thinly and stamp out 14 circles 6 cm/2^1/$_2$ inches wide. Set these on the buttercream to cover the top of each cake.

Roll out the green sugarpaste thinly and cut into narrow strips 2.5 cm/1 inch wide. Take a cocktail stick and roll this back and forth to flute up the edges of the sugarpaste. Cut the fluted strips into graduated layers to make a triangular tree shape and press onto the cakes. Decorate with edible silver balls. Keep for 3 days in an airtight container.

Christmas Pudding Cupcakes

c

Makes 14–18

125 g/4 oz butter
125 g/4 oz soft dark
muscovado sugar
2 medium eggs, beaten
225 g/8 oz self-raising flour
1 tsp ground mixed spice
finely grated zest and 1 tbsp
juice from 1 orange
1 tbsp black treacle
350 g/12 oz mixed dried fruit

To decorate

3 tbsp sieved apricot glaze
(see page 64)
225 g/8 oz almond paste
(see page 62)
450 g/1 lb ready-to-roll sugarpaste
brown, red, green and yellow paste
food colourings

Preheat the oven to 180°C/350°F/Gas Mark 4. Line one or two 12-hole bun trays with 14–18 foil fairy-cake cases. Beat the butter and sugar together, then beat in the eggs, adding 1 teaspoon flour with each addition. Sift in the remaining flour and the spice, add the orange zest and juice, treacle and dried fruit to the bowl and fold together. Spoon into the cases and bake for about 30 minutes. Leave to cool in the trays for 15 minutes, then turn out to cool on a wire rack. Store undecorated in an airtight container for up to 4 weeks, or freeze.

To decorate, trim the top of each cake level, then brush with apricot glaze. Roll out the almond paste and cut out circles 6 cm/21/2 inches wide. Place a disc on top of each cake and press level. Leave to dry for 24 hours. Dust a clean, flat surface with icing sugar. Colour half the sugarpaste brown, roll out thinly and cut out circles 6 cm/2^1/$_2$ inches wide. Place on top of the almond paste and press level. Colour the remaining sugarpaste cream or pale yellow, mould into a fluted disc and press on top for custard. Colour the sugarpaste scraps green and red and shape into holly leaves and berries. Keep for 1 week in an airtight container.

White Chocolate Christmas Cakes

Makes 12–16

150 g/5 oz butter, softened
150 g/5 oz caster sugar
150 g/5 oz self-raising flour
3 medium eggs, beaten
1 tsp vanilla extract
1 tbsp milk
75 g/3 oz white chocolate,
finely grated

To decorate

250 g/9 oz white
chocolate, chopped
16 holly leaves, cleaned
and dried
1 batch buttercream
(see page 60)
icing sugar, for dusting

Preheat the oven to 180°C/350°F/Gas Mark 4. Line one or two 12-hole bun trays with 12–16 foil cases. Place the butter and sugar in a bowl, then sift in the flour. Add the eggs to the bowl with the vanilla extract and milk and beat until smooth. Fold in the grated white chocolate, then spoon into the cases, filling them three-quarters full. Bake for about 18 minutes. Turn out to cool on a wire rack.

To decorate, melt the white chocolate in a heatproof bowl standing over a pan of barely simmering water. Use one third of the melted chocolate to paint the undersides of the holly leaves and leave to set for 30 minutes in the refrigerator. Spread one third of the chocolate out onto a clean plastic board. When almost set, make into curls by pulling a sharp knife through the chocolate at an angle until the chocolate curls away from the knife. Stir the remaining cooled chocolate into the buttercream and chill for 15 minutes. Swirl each cupcake with buttercream, then press on the white chocolate curls. Peel the holly leaves away from the chocolate and carefully place on top of the cupcakes. Dust with icing sugar before serving. Keep for 2 days in the refrigerator.

Templates for Sugarpaste Shapes

LARGE HEART

SMALL HEART

HOLLY

MEDIUM HEART

On these pages, you will find templates for some of the icing shapes as used in this book. Templates such as these are handy if you do not have a selection of metal cutters. Just trace the pattern you want onto a sheet of clear greaseproof paper or nonslick baking parchment. Roll out the sugarpaste thinly, then position the traced pattern over the icing. Mark over the pattern with the tip of a small, sharp knife or a pin. Remove the paper and cut out the marked-on pattern with a small, sharp knife. Voilà!

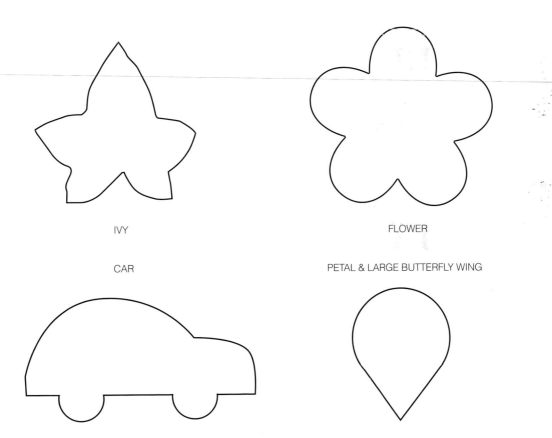

IVY

FLOWER

CAR

PETAL & LARGE BUTTERFLY WING

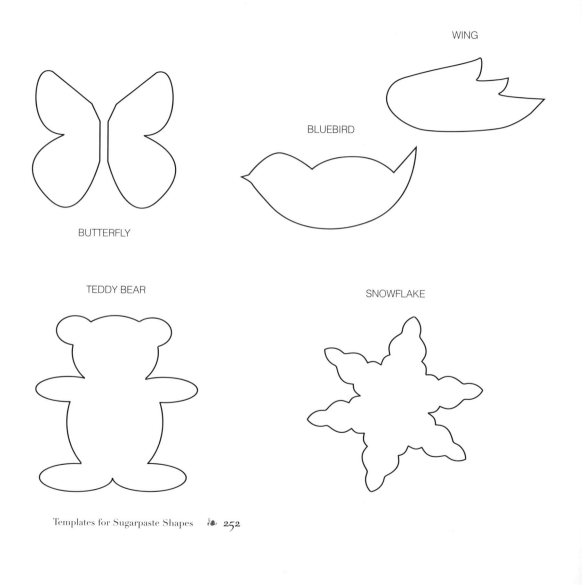

WING

BLUEBIRD

BUTTERFLY

TEDDY BEAR

SNOWFLAKE

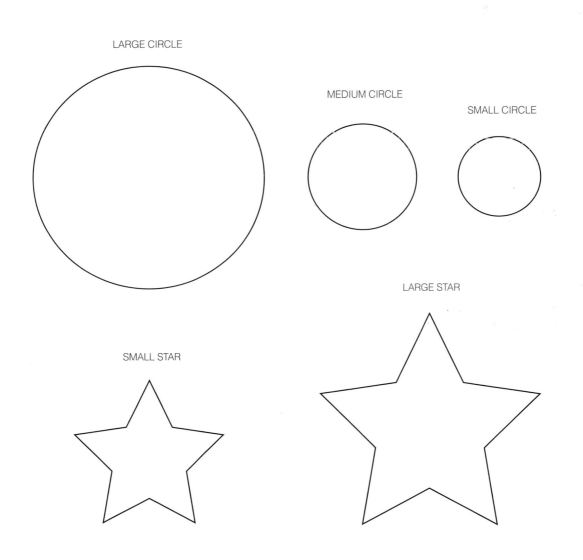

LARGE CIRCLE

MEDIUM CIRCLE

SMALL CIRCLE

LARGE STAR

SMALL STAR

Index

Index